SHADES *of*
PUBLIC
FINANCE

VOLUME ONE
Illicit Bankruptcies,

Innovative Municipal Bonds, and

Why the Patriots Didn't Move to Hartford

Richard Land Sigal

DUDLEY COURT PRESS
SONOITA, AZ

Published in the United States of America by
Dudley Court Press
PO Box 102 Sonoita, AZ 85637
www.DudleyCourtPress.com

Cover and interior design by Dunn+Associates, www.Dunn-Design.com

Publisher's Cataloging-in-Publication Data
Names: Sigal, Richard Land, author.
Title: Shades of public finance / Richard Land Sigal.
Description: Sonoita : Dudley Court Press, LLC, [2020]
Contents: vol. 1. Illicit bankrutpcies, innovative municipal bonds, and why the patriots didn't move to Hartford
Contents vol. 2. More insider stories of the municipal bonds that built America.
Identifiers: ISBN: 978-1-940013-66-4 (v. 1 : paperback) | 978-1-940013-73-2 (v.2 : paperback)
978-1-940013-61-9 (v.1 : ebook) | 978-1-940013-62-6 (v. 2 : ebook)
978-1-940013-74-9 (v.1 : audio) | 978-1-940013-75-6 (v. 2 : audio)
LCCN: 2019921137 (v. 1) | 2019921092 (v. 2)
Subjects: LCSH: Municipal bonds—Law and legislation--United States. | Bond market—United States.
Bond market—United States—History. | Municipal finance—United States. | Local finance—United States.
BISAC: BUSINESS & ECONOMICS / Public Finance. | BUSINESS & ECONOMICS / Finance / General.
BUSINESS & ECONOMICS / Economic History. | BUSINESS & ECONOMICS / Skills.
Classification: LCC: KF6775 .S54 2020 | DDC: 346.73/0922--dc23

Look for other books in this series at your favorite bookseller
or at www.DudleyCourtPress.com

CONTENTS

D uring the period after World War II, public finance emerged as the practical and effective investment resource tool for government to expand and improve the infrastructure in the United States. Among other things, modern infrastructure includes highways, airports, bridges, tunnels, parks, clean water supply, sewage treatment, power generation, solid waste disposal, government office facilities, and sometimes stadiums and arenas. Public finance represents a key economic anchor for any region and is essential to enable, sustain, and enhance living conditions. State and municipal bonds—interest exempt from federal income tax and highly rated as a safe and prudent investment—became the market that attracted both wealthy Americans and trust funds to provide the capital necessary for these projects. How? The bonds give a yield incentive without default risk. The bonds were secured by real estate taxes; by revenues from the toll roads; by assessments or charges for sewer, water supply, and solid waste disposal service; or by concession payments under public-private partnerships.

Shades of Public Finance features the inside story behind the accomplishments and failures of many public finance bond issues and public officials. By providing an insider's account of financings by state and local governments over the most recent six decades, *Shades of Public Finance* provides lessons from which those interested in public funding can learn. As such, it's an enlightening and essential resource for every citizen. Finding the "ways and means" of financing important projects while maintaining state and local solvency in this century is imperative to making the necessary improvements and expansions of the many kinds of infrastructure serving the public.

I have been one of few lawyers practicing public finance for more than fifty years. I had the rare privilege of starting at a firm that carved out this specialty—a firm with the master builder Robert Moses as a client. Both New York City and New York State remain indebted to him and the authorities he chaired that planned, financed, built, and operated the infrastructures serving its citizens today. They include managing the Power Authority with its magnificent power plants in Niagara Falls; building the Robert F. Kennedy Triborough, Throgs Neck, Whitestone, Henry Hudson, and Verrazzano bridges; and developing Jones Beach park and millions of apartments owned by the NYC Housing Authority. They also include building the original Shea Stadium—inspiring Major League Baseball to allow the New York Mets to replace the relocated Dodgers and Giants—and Moses's last project, the New York World's Fair in 1964.

In addition to my firsthand knowledge of the legacy of Robert Moses and his counsel, Lewis Delafield, I had the privilege of being an associate and then a partner in a firm of professionals who were icons of public finance. I introduce a few of them here.

Ike Russell was known as Mr. Turnpike because he drafted the revenue bond structure to finance the toll roads and toll bridges from Maine to Maryland. He developed the innovative tripartite interstate compact arrangement for DC, Maryland, and Virginia to build the District of Columbia transit system. He was also the creative mind behind uniquely expanding Manhattan with the rock excavations from the first two World Trade Towers and building Battery Park City.

Chuck Kades, once the aide de camp for General Douglas MacArthur, wrote the pacifism provisions into the Japanese Constitution and, after World War II, became the leading tax lawyer for the entire public finance industry.[1]

Frank Wood first shared offices with Thomas Dewey and "did well" when his former office mate became governor of New York. He did even better when Mr. Dewey became the named managing partner of Dewey Ballantine. Despite his many public official contacts, he chose to not practice public finance law, leaving that public service specialty to Mr. Wood.

I worked with these professionals, investment bankers, governors, state and local fiscal officers, and my amazing contemporary partners. From them, I gained experience on issues that, today, are major historical breakthroughs and regularly applied precedents in structuring debt instruments for building state and municipal infrastructure and for balancing budgets during periods of fiscal stress.

I am honored to share aspects of this experience with you in this book, *Shades of Public Finance: Illicit Bankruptcies, Innovative Municipal Bonds, and Why the Patriots Didn't Move to Hartford* (Volume 1) and its companion book, *More Shades of Public Finance: Insider Stories of the Municipal Bonds That Built America* (Volume 2).

Shades of Public Finance provides you with a path showing the history of public finance and, by example, suggests the extension of that path for recovering a sound public fiscal administration in the United States. Unlike a traditional textbook, it teaches the lessons of public financing by using example transactions to provide the facts from which the principles of public finance are pictured.

This book started as a simple collection of complex public finance transactions and programs to educate people on the contributions of the tax-exempt bond market to our daily lives. The municipal bond market in the United States has been successful in attracting investors because of two factors: (1) bonds are exempt from federal taxation on interest income, and (2) hardly any bond issues have gone unpaid due to municipal bankruptcies or default/nonpayment. That means a multibillion-dollar market developed composed primarily of wealthy individuals (or investment funds attracting wealthy investors) who would buy state and local bond issues at attractive low interest rates.

Consider this unique governmental system in which the Tenth Amendment of the U.S. Constitution reserves to the states all powers that aren't explicitly assigned to the federal government. Thus, the states are sovereigns, and the municipalities within them are political subdivisions. Ever since the imposition of the federal income tax, immunity from income taxation on the interest on municipal bonds has been preserved. (In Volume 2, Chapter 12: What is Arbitrage? relates several exceptions to the tax-exempt feature—primarily federal legislation curbing tax-exempt borrowings with the primary purpose of taking advantage of the tax differential—so called "arbitrage.") This means the proceeds of tax-exempt interest bonds are invested in obligations guaranteed by the federal government priced at higher taxable interest rates, including U.S. Treasury bills. The exceptions to such tax exemptions include obvious public policy distortions such as bond financing (at tax-exempt rates) (1) of multimillion-dollar manufacturing plants or office buildings for lease to private corporations, (2) to make mortgage loans for financing homes for high-income families, or (3) issued as bearer bonds rather than bonds registered in the owner's name. That last point became law once the U.S. Treasury persuaded Congress that bearer bonds had become a drug trade and money-laundering currency.

Recently, however, the perception of the bond market has changed because of the *business* bankruptcy decision made in Orange County and particularly the *political* bankruptcy decisions in Detroit and Puerto Rico. (See Chapters 3, 4, and 5.) These two decisions have polluted traditional principles of fiscal governance, breaking the bounds of traditional and proven public finance practices.[2] Presidents, governors, mayors, corporate bankruptcy lawyers, financial advisors, and even federal judges are now blowing off those principles that public finance professionals know and were taught to respect. This includes the benefits derived from the synergy between state and local issuers and between investment bankers and insurers. Many of the elected officials, including Republican Governor Rick Snyder in Michigan (2011–2016; in respect to Detroit) and Democratic President Barack Obama (2008–2016; in respect to Puerto Rico) and U.S. Treasury appointees were "badly advised." Worse, they were blabbering corporate hyperboles as they went along. They coated their policy pronouncements with rhetoric that lacked public finance backup, precedent, and vision. Worse than that, they were victimized by officious bankruptcy lawyers and financial consultants and did not listen to public finance experts who had successfully weathered governmental fiscal crises before Orange County, Detroit, and Puerto Rico. Fiscal crises and successful recoveries occurred in the 1970s and 1980s in New York City and Yonkers, New York; Bridgeport and Waterbury, Connecticut; Philadelphia, Pittsburgh, and Scranton, Pennsylvania; and more recently, in Rhode Island[3]; Hartford, Connecticut; and Atlantic City, New Jersey. Most surprisingly, the Obama administration and Congress ignored its own precedent that chose consensus restructuring over bankruptcy for the District of Columbia. That structure of fiscal oversight and refunding of debt was modeled on the Carey legislation in New York.

I liken the chaos occurring in Puerto Rico to a hurricane, with the resulting fiscal damage to the public finance bond market scattered everywhere. We are only now beginning to understand the ramifications.

Willingness to Pay Full Value

Crucial to this book that criticizes current municipal bankruptcy politics and policy is appreciating the fact that public finance's bedrock principle was established by Alexander Hamilton, creator of the U.S. financial system and first Secretary of the Treasury (1789–1795). Hamilton insisted that government was obligated to honor its *faith and credit* as imprinted on the dollar bill.

As *the* example, during the American Revolution of 1765–1783, troops in the North were paid in dollars. However, banks and merchants were not confident that the Americans would beat the British, so those soldiers could not use their paychecks in dollars at their full value. However, speculators were willing to take a financial risk. They regularly discounted these dollars by 10 to 40 percent. The money speculators of 1770s are the hedge fund managers of today.

By comparison, leaders in the South had better wherewithal to pay their fighting troops than those in the North. Regardless of the outcome of the conflict, the value of the cotton economy was recognized, allowing troops from those Southern states to be paid in gold. But at the end of the Revolutionary War, James Madison and Thomas Jefferson, two of the founding fathers from Southern states, refused to have the American Congress honor the dollar's value. They argued that speculators should be paid no more than the discounted rate that the speculators themselves had paid. Hamilton refused to accept that. He held that the United States had pledged its faith and credit to pay full value—one hundred cents—on the dollar. In their negotiations on this point, Hamilton offered to move the capital from New York City to DC, a "southern" city. As a result of that negotiation, Madison and Jefferson honored the pledge to pay one hundred cents on the dollar.

Bedrock of Governmental Finance Until . . .

The principle of *honoring the obligation to pay full value on governmental debt* became the bedrock of governmental finance and policy until June 29, 2016.[4] That's when the U.S. Treasury guilefully persuaded members of Congress to abandon that principle in Puerto Rico. They passed a federal statute known as PROMESA, which authorized and directed the Commonwealth of Puerto Rico to be subjected to a special federal statutory bankruptcy process. Orange County chipped away at this bedrock principle too, but as discussed in Chapter 3, the circumstances of that business choice to declare bankruptcy is now understood to have been a mistake. Therefore, it already has not been and will not become a precedent.

The big-picture public finance market risk previewed in Puerto Rico is that federal legislation could pass and permit any state to file for bankruptcy under Chapter 9 of the Federal Bankruptcy Act (at its option) without violating the Tenth Amendment of the U.S. Constitution. Unfortunately, in 2016, there was no political leader comparable to Alexander

Hamilton to instruct the officials. And no public finance experts were invited to Washington, DC, to convince the politicians of their folly. (The explanation of why this happened is a major topic of Chapters 4 and 5.)

Historically, the fledgling state of Alaska recognized the importance of the public finance market based on its fiscal response to a 1965 earthquake. That's when its leaders explored the fundamentals of public finance and laid the foundation of the state's bond credit that continues today. (See Chapter 13.)

In 1975, New York City was fortunate to have leaders, particularly the governor of New York State, Hugh Carey (1975–1982), who recognized that bankruptcy was not an acceptable choice. (See Chapter 1.) The state coordinated a consensus for special legislation to restructure and extend the debt with the state's unions, bondholders, banks, and taxpayers on resolving the issues in a constructive manner. This action sidelined others, including the then mayor of New York City, who was considering the bankruptcy option and had a corporate bankruptcy counsel with documents ready to file. Similar constructive coordination in Connecticut, Pennsylvania, and Rhode Island also can be reported as an endorsement of the Hamiltonian principle.

But in 2015, officials of the U.S. Treasury viewed founding father Alexander Hamilton and Governor Hugh Carey as "old school," taking the municipal market into the darkness of bankruptcy and repudiation of debt.

State and local government leaders and their counsel as well as all federal government leaders should be reminded there is "no cotton" to sell to back their bonds—nor cars, nor any other commodity or product. They must recognize the willingness to *pay debt when due* as being the key principle of market acceptance for state and local bonds.

Public Finance as an Investment Resource Tool[5]

The great achievements of public finance in the twentieth century were built through bond mechanisms. These include New York City's third water tunnel—the biggest New York City public works project in history. This water tunnel, which took fifty years to complete, is sixty miles long and about five hundred feet below street level. It brings snow melt from upstate New York through Westchester and the Bronx to Manhattan and Queens. (See Chapter 11.)

Likewise, tax-exempt bonds made possible the District of Columbia's transit system, which is a commuter solution achieved through an interstate agreement among Maryland, Virginia, and DC. Other projects are the three-lane Connecticut Turnpike that connects Interstate 95 in New York with Massachusetts and Rhode Island, and Alaska's recovery from the great earthquake of 1964. Also in New York City, public bonds built Battery Park City, which is the residential/office complex constructed on landfill rock from the excavation for the two World Trade Center Towers. (See Chapter 13.) You'll read unique stories behind these and other bond issues in this book.

Shades of Public Finance is full of political intrigue, deal-making, and planning compromises. The historic accounts involve colorful and ambitious characters in business and government, including presidents, governors, mayors, and professionals in law, business, and finance. Studying the past success of public finance of public infrastructure does not, however, provide a simple template from which current government entities can operate. Rather, as the public demands increasingly more expensive governmental infrastructure, it has engendered an evolving complex field of legal and governmental coordination and contract security.

Today's Landscape

Supposedly, the political landscape was changed by the election of Donald Trump, a man whose *raison d'etre* is building infrastructure.[6] But the fiscal picture he inherited does not provide a clear finance landscape on how to do what he claims he wants to do—to rebuild our roads and utilities and expand our capital public facilities to meet the needs of our populace. To do that, he and his successors will undoubtedly count on the municipal bond market to participate in financing those public works as it has in the past.[7]

However, in this twenty-first century, the two investment incentives of tax exemption and safety from bond default or bankruptcy that attract investing in municipal bonds are being endangered. The U.S. Treasury continues its relentless attack to curb or eliminate tax exemption on municipal bonds. Passing the 2017–18 Tax Act eliminated what's called "advanced refundings." But for that statute, bonds would be issued in today's market at far lower interest rates to take out high interest rate bonds before their maturity. This would provide significant tax savings to state and municipal taxpayers. As discussed in Chapter 11 in Volume 2, the U.S. Treasury continues to refuse to understand that reduced interest rates mean lower levels of state and local taxes are required to pay debt service and, accordingly, more money is available for taxpayers to spend. The U.S. Treasury also continues to argue that shutting down tax exemption on state and municipal bonds results in increased federal tax receipts from the wealthy while ignoring the proven fact that those investors will simply shift to another tax shelter. Worse, the U.S. Treasury refuses to acknowledge that eliminating this tax exemption will result in huge tax increases at state and local levels to cover the higher interest rates on those bonds.

Headlines about defaults and bankruptcy in Puerto Rico and Detroit, the most recent examples, suggest breaches of confidence in the safety of municipal bonds and erode the attractiveness of the public finance market. As a result, certain states with recurring years of budget-balancing problems are on the watch lists of rating agencies and investors. Phrases like repudiation of debt obligations, creditor haircuts, and cramdown on bondholders have crept into the lexicon of public finance.

Moreover, a significant new force of creditors has become a claimant to parity treatment or even a preference over bondholders. They are former and current state and municipal employees who have vested contractual rights to pensions and health benefits. Added to the high levels of bonded debt is the ever-increasing unfunded liability of these benefits. (A May 2019 Forbes article provides an excellent summation of the threat to state economies posed by past failures to properly budget for pension and health benefits on an annual basis in accordance with accrual accounting standards.[8])

It should be noted that municipal bonds are traded in a multi-billion-dollar market. So despite threats of default (or, frankly, because of threats of default), there is money to be made. As will be shown in Chapter 4 on the Puerto Rican fiscal debacle, certain buyers of Senior COFINA bonds and their consultants made millions in smart trades and success fees.[9]

Currently, many states and municipalities are encountering budget balancing stress. This is resulting from (1) escalating contractual obligations to employees for pension and health care benefits and (2) increasing bonded indebtedness for essential capital improvements and, during recent recessions, to fund general fund deficits. In most states and municipalities, the political fact is that increasing taxes cannot be the answer. Thus remains the question of whether an insolvency process for a state or a bankruptcy under Chapter 9 of the Federal Bankruptcy Act for a municipality (and, at its option, for a state) is ever the right option. In Orange County, the business decision was YES. In Detroit and Puerto Rico, the political answer was YES. But these answers reflect the wrong option. Recently, in the Atlantic City and Hartford fiscal stress cases, the answer was NO. Why? Because the state governments of New Jersey and Connecticut, respectively, interceded with proven oversight supervision (NJ) and traditional state credit enhancement (CT). Rhode Island is an excellent example of how to honor the obligation to pay in full the debt service on bonds when due even when municipal bankruptcy looms. The state passed legislation permitting its municipalities to file for bankruptcy. However, the statute excludes bond debt from the bankruptcy process and thus protects both credit ratings and the ability to borrow for essential capital improvements.

Lest you think that this book is limited to rebuffing the pro-motors—from the corporate and sovereign segments of finance, of municipal bankruptcy—let me say it is *not*. By exposing the shady sides of the Orange Country, Detroit, and Puerto Rico executive decisions and suggesting adjustments to the bankruptcy provisions under Chapter 9 of the Federal Bankruptcy Act, I anticipate that you as taxpayers will understand the issues sufficiently to counter such bad behavior in your state or municipality.

Other chapters are intended to educate you about the wide variety of fiscal issues that confront state and local governments every day. The case studies illustrate the creativity of elected and appointed officials in resolving those issues—and should inspire you to become smartly supportive in your community.

PART ONE

Why Bankruptcy Does Not Work for Governments

CHAPTER 1

New York City:
A Billion-Dollar Opinion

*If you're unfamiliar with state and local finance law, you
may consider a career in counseling government officials
to be routine and repetitive. However, boring paperwork
wasn't what I experienced in my career. Compared to the
glamour of the corporate finance, legal, and investment
banking careers of my college and law school classmates,
I found that I preferred the excitement of contributing
to good government. I did this by counseling governors,
state treasurers, and other state and local leaders and by
developing finance statutes and programs.*

came to appreciate my practice at Hawkins.[1] My work there was
not only diverse, interesting, and innovative; it was based on the
pursuit of public purposes and raising money for infrastructure
improvements that would truly make people's lives better. In 1964,
I started at Hawkins and earned $7,500 a year. By comparison, my
contemporaries at Cravath, a leading corporate law firm, received the
going rate of $7,800. Louis Auchincloss was Hawkins' hiring partner,
who also authored fiction books on New York society. He offered that
counseling government didn't allow one to bill as high as those who

worked for corporate clients; however, doing good for the public was an intangible benefit—better than chasing big bucks as happens in the corporate finance practice.

Over the years, mergers and acquisitions, hostile takeovers, junk and mortgage-backed bonds, Enron, and the like consumed the corporate finance and venture capital legal practices in large, complicated deals—for higher salaries and routinely longer hours. But most of us at Hawkins were comfortable with the public finance practice with its occasional all-nighters and lower level of remuneration.

In particular, I enjoyed structuring the innovations required for several programs that developed over the past fifty years in almost every state. These programs included tax-exempt Clean Water Bonds[2] leveraging federal and state grants, Industrial Revenue Bonds, Housing Mortgage Revenue Bonds,[3] Pollution Control Bonds,[4] Private Public Partnership bonds, state, and municipal fiscal restructuring bonds, and Tobacco Settlement–Turbo Charged bonds.[5] Working on these programs in many states set me up in a national public finance practice that proved to be highly satisfying over the decades.

Starting in 1964 and for several years after, I became proficient in basic New York local finance law. I worked on financings for counties such as Erie, Rockland, Broome, Suffolk, and Nassau as well as the cities of Buffalo, Syracuse, New York, Binghamton, Glen Cove, and Long Beach, as well as the towns of Hempstead, Clarkstown, and Amherst.

Historically, Hawkins had bond counsel relationship retainers with these government entities. It also had clients at the state level with Lewis Delafield as *the* bond counsel for Robert Moses. Moses created and chaired a number of authorities, including the New York Power Authority, Triborough Bridge and Tunnel Authority, and Jones Beach Parkway Authority. (*The Power Broker: Robert Moses and the Fall of New York*[6] by Robert Caro spotlights the good and bad of Robert Moses as a public servant.)

Rapid Growth in the 1960s

For me, being a lawyer in the firm that represented Moses provided a legacy of precedents, prestige, and profit second to none. The 1960s saw rapid growth in the suburbs of New York in Rockland County, including its towns of Clarkstown, Haverstraw, and Ramapo. Every month, a call came in to start the proceedings for creating a sewer district to finance the construction of interceptor sewers and laterals. With septic tanks no longer allowed, this meant newly developed housing subdivisions had to be connected to a sewage treatment plant. Thus, I learned about timely public notice. Accordingly, I learned that an assessment is for improving real property. It must be preceded by a process of notice and include a determination of all who benefit. This is true even if the location is just an open lot with promising potential. Also, rates and charges were permitted if a reasonable way of charging for use was established. Clearly, metering of water was permitted, but charging by proxy based on the number of toilets was okay, too.

A property tax is levied for a general benefit such as financing a town's municipal hall. But it could also be permitted to finance the construction of water or sewer facilities if the politicians prefer levying property taxes to pay debt service on the bond rather than assessing or charging for such services.

As the cost of construction increased, more municipalities turned to rates and charges rather than property taxes. (See Chapter 11 that discusses creating the New York City Water Authority.) When a bond proposal was put on the agenda at public meetings, its complicated, technical, and controversial legal processes caused a lot of people to turn out to complain or understand the issues. As a young lawyer and issuer's bond counsel, I attended many evening meetings where I learned about local politics and policy. There, I honed my skills in responding to the many questions asked by those in attendance.

My research put me into the dustbin of recorded minutes of state constitutional conventions. There, I learned the background and reasons for debt limits, tax limits, and when and why some municipalities had to have a referendum or a permissive referendum subject to a filing of signatures to force an actual referendum. I also learned when and how an assessment district or village could be formed and why New York had many restrictive constitutional finance provisions while Connecticut had only one.[7]

"Faith and Credit Pledge"

In addition, I learned that, in New York, a municipality could issue bonds only as a general obligation for the payment, of which it pledged its "faith and credit." That imprecise phrase carried enormous security significance in the public finance bond market. It meant that issuing bonds constituted a contract. This was the municipality's general pledge to make available not only the revenues from an unlimited real estate levy, but all revenue resources, such as those from sales tax.

I also learned that similar sections of the state constitution restricted the state itself, and that any general obligation state bond needed approval by the voters. One of the primary reasons the state had so many public authorities was to circumvent those direct constitutional restrictions on state debt.

Our Role in the New York City Fiscal Crisis

Despite having such detailed expertise in New York public finance law, nothing had prepared me for what became perhaps the singular achievement of my fifty-plus years of public finance practice. It occurred in my eleventh year of practice, in 1971. I conceived and drafted the bond security structure that prevented the New York City bankruptcy in 1975.

New York City faced a fiscal crisis in 1975.[8] Governor Hugh Carey was advised to retain my firm, Hawkins, to structure a new bond approach to avoid the necessity of the city filing for bankruptcy.

As the lead partner on New York finance law and steeped in practicing general obligation bond counsel law, I researched the history and constitutional financial cases in point (not only in New York but elsewhere). My confidence never wavered, despite knowing the enormous downside if I were wrong. I recommended repealing the city sales tax and permitting a state sales tax in the city to be pledged by a separate legal entity (eventually known as MAC, the Municipal Assistance Corporation).

Early on, my partner, Don Robinson, reviewed the structure and agreed to it; another partner, Gerry Fernandez, thought I was right. And Eric Petersen, my team associate and later partner, revised the office memorandum to affirm we were on certain constitutional grounds and that litigation challenging the structure would be decided in our favor.

The legal analysis went like this: The finance provisions of the New York State Constitution stated explicitly that the only tax revenue a bondholder of New York City was entitled to as security (as a matter of contract law) was the real property tax. The legislature had the explicit constitutional "duty" to safeguard the credit of its municipalities. It followed, then, that the legislature had the authority to repeal the existing city sales tax. If that city sales tax was not repealed, it would have had to be available to pay the city's general obligation and could not be pledged to other debts. The legislation then could replace that tax immediately with a state sales tax in the city so that a public authority could pledge that tax. As the security for its bonds, that tax would pay off the billions of dollars of notes previously issued by the city, which would go into default—*unless this securitization of the newly designated New York State sales tax was successful.*

To repeat: Because the city was required on every bond to "pledge its faith and credit," the city itself could not issue a revenue bond. Why? Because that "faith and credit" pledge meant all the taxing resources of the city must be available to pay its general obligation bonds. It also meant a pledge of the sales taxes to secure a revenue bond and not others would contradict that requirement.

With our approach, the security for general obligation bondholders would not be adversely affected. Those bonds still had the security benefit of the real property tax. In addition, an income tax and other revenue sources were also available, allowing the city to honor its "faith and credit" pledge. Most important, the maturing notes of the city would be paid with the MAC bonds.

It also became clear that the general obligation bonds were being protected from the only other option the city had—to file for bankruptcy. My analysis (backed by that memorandum of law) was based on relevant provisions of the state constitution and the legislative history of the constitutional convention discussing the adoption of those provisions.

The Hawkins firm rendered an approving opinion for the first billion-dollar bond issue in history, to be issued by the newly created Municipal Assistance Corporation (MAC, a new state authority).[9]

Hawkins was New York's unqualified leading law firm on public finance. Every counsel to the underwriters—Davis Polk, Shearman & Sterling, Cleary Gottlieb, Dewey Ballantine, Cravath, Milbank, and White & Case—counseled with their financial clients who were engaged to underwrite and sell the bonds. They declared that our analysis of New York law was correct and could be relied upon even in light of litigation filed during the marketing period challenging the validity of the legal structure.

Legislation was passed to create the Municipal Assistance Corporation Act—the MAC Act—and to authorize bonds to be secured by a new "state" sales tax levied only in the city. After that, Don Robinson and I worked almost twenty hours a day for several weeks. We put the documents in place for this new issuer and met with underwriters and corporate counsel on the covenants, structural details, and disclosure matters related to this billion-dollar offering. We wanted to assure bondholders that this structure would secure not only the first billion-dollar deal but many billions more. This was needed to pay off maturing notes and bond out the city's general fund deficit resulting from reduced federal revenue streams.

Two Rewarding Events

Of the hundreds of day-to-day events, two are most rewarding for me to remember. The first was working with Jack Bigel, the financial advisor to the unions whose members were employed by New York City. Victor Gotbaum led those unions. I was assigned to convince these two gentlemen that the unions should not only publicly support an effort to prevent the city from filing for bankruptcy but that they should also invest their pension funds in the purchase of a substantial portion of this first billion-dollar issue.

The reason was straightforward. We knew Michael Cook, then of Weil, Gotshal & Manges, was counseling Mayor Abraham Beame about filing for bankruptcy. Strategically, we needed to be sure the unions would not push the mayor to order Cook to file either *before* or *after* the first billion-dollar issue. If it occurred *before*, of course, there would be no bond issue. But if *after*, the bond proceeds paying off existing noteholders could have been deemed a "preference" and spoiled the whole process of recovery.

No law firm including Hawkins could offer an opinion on the outcome of the MAC pledge of the sales tax in such a city bankruptcy; hence, the bond issue might have been considered unmarketable. But if the various unions representing city employees invested their pension funds in the bonds, it would signal the union's real-time support for the first (and many more) bond issues. In that way, it would politically minimize support for the bankruptcy option.

The biggest issue three of us discussed over two consecutive all-night sessions was the prudence of the unions investing in these bonds to preclude a bankruptcy filing. Finally, these leaders were convinced a bankruptcy alternative would put the pensions of the union employees in a potential subordinated position to the out-standing noteholders. The outstanding notes came with an explicit state constitutional contract pledge of the city's real estate tax and its faith and credit pledge to apply all other city revenues or all other taxes to pay the maturing notes. Also, President Gerald Ford had made it clear that his administration would not bail out New York City government or its noteholders.[10]

My expertise on the New York Constitution bolstered my advocacy. I knew the history of the so-called "first lien" constitutional pledge as well as the underlying "pledge of faith and credit" to include all other revenue resources such as income taxes. The 1938 New York Consti-tutional Convention had made it clear that the key to self-sufficiency and service to residents is to make sure the state and its municipalities always had access to bond markets for capital improvements. Accord-ingly, the New York local finance state constitutional provisions include several security provisions protecting a preference for bondholders.

The city would be required by state constitutional law to set aside its first revenues to pay bond and note indebtedness if the city defaulted. It was "jump ball" at best whether the unions could over-come such application in bankruptcy. Therefore, it was prudent for the unions to support the debt restructuring by buying a significant number of MAC bonds.

Jack Bigel, impressed with my legal advocacy, asked for my help on some ERISA issues that worried the unions. My response—"What is ERISA?"—was met with a smile. Bigel then understood I was only a smart public finance lawyer. To this day, I have to look up the full title of that acronym, which is the Employee Retirement Income Security Act of 1974.

A second honor was being the fourth man in the room with newly elected Governor Carey; Judge Rifkind of Paul, Weiss, and then-chairman of MAC; Felix Rohatyn, financier from Lazard Frères. They discussed imposing a moratorium on payment of New York City notes and bonds to provide more time to work on the MAC's first offering. There had been a moratorium imposed by the United States during the depression in the 1930s on payments of home mortgages, which had been upheld by the Blaisdell case in the U.S. Supreme Court. Judge Rifkind cited this as *the* supporting case for the state of New York to go forward. The sense was that it was a temporary delay and would not be deemed a debt default under an emergency exception. I cautioned, "There might be other options, but this one might very well be unconstitutional as an impairment of the 'faith and credit' contract under the New York State Constitution. Hawkins could not give an opinion that it would be a valid exercise of state power. Maybe closing banks, as was done in the depression to avoid presentation of the debt for payment, could be a better precedent."

My mentor and senior partner Ike Russell confirmed my advice. In fact, he wrote a personal letter to our client, Governor Carey, stating he did not realize he held his law license from a "banana republic." (This pejorative term is associated with South American governments that refuse to pay their lawfully incurred debts.) Russell classified the moratorium on payment of debt service as a repudiation of debt.

Despite my concern, the legislation was introduced. It passed, and a moratorium on payment was imposed on the payment of those notes. Two years later, the highest court in New York held that moratorium was unconstitutional for exactly the reason I had stated in that earlier meeting.[11]

From Judge Rifkind, I learned he had enough law experience to make a plausible case for such counseling. The time it took to litigate the issue gave the working group an opportunity to complete and market the MAC bonds, paying off the notes in default, including accrued interest. Indeed, the outcome of the case itself was not as critical as providing us with that time, and because the marketing of MAC bonds over the next several years was so successful, the "technical default" did not result in any interest penalty on city borrowings. In fact, the decision by New York's highest court upholding the meaning of the "faith and credit pledge" to exclude even an emergency exception was regularly cited by the rating agencies as the city's ratings improved over the years that followed.

CHAPTER 2

Yonkers:
Two Near-Bankruptcies

Many cities are managed by a city manager or chief executive officer (CEO) appointed by and responsible to the city council. Others have as the CEO an elected mayor who executes actions approved by the city council. In my view, both forms of governing work fine; effectiveness of either depends on the personalities involved. The city of Yonkers has tried both forms without particular success, probably because its city council is composed of a member from each ward. That's when everything becomes subject to logrolling, as this chapter explains.

In 1975, the city of Yonkers had accrued a general fund deficit that could not be balanced by any reasonable tax increase. The local finance law precluded bonding to fund a deficit unless authorized under a special act of the state legislature. Like New York City, Yonkers's leaders were considering several options to address this deficit, including bankruptcy.

Also like New York City, Yonkers had accrued a fund deficit because it anticipated federal revenue sharing in annually increasing amounts. Instead, as that federal program was being phased out and annual grants routinely reduced, Yonkers had been left with programmatic service commitments. That meant the general fund deficit was accumulating for each of these years due to federal revenue sharing being less than expected. In retrospect, it became clear that the start of any benefit program based on annual congressional appropriation of discretionary federal grants should be structured to expire and employees fired or transferred to openings elsewhere if the federal government sharing stopped.

Funding Issues in Yonkers

In 1975, Yonkers was managed by a strong form of city manager and a titular-only mayor. Many thought that's why the budget was a mess, having missed the programmatic federal decision to reduce annual revenue sharing.

My analysis was this: The city used the ward system for election of members to city council without any members elected at large. Therefore, passing any funding increase or decrease required ward-by-ward deals (known as "logrolling")—and even then, getting a unanimous vote was unheard of. Therefore, reduction of particular programs meant finding candidates for such reductions in equal amounts from each ward—not an easy task.

City Manager Vinny Castaldo was a rough, tough guy who was also a politically savvy and serious civil servant. He could cajole enough votes to run the city well. However, balancing the budget by cuts or tax increases after the federal government had reduced revenue sharing went beyond his bullying and deal-making abilities.

Counting on ongoing annual revenues from federal grants, Yonkers had hired new employees for certain programs. But it wasn't practical to consider a reduction in workforce parallel with the reduction in grants, at least not in the city environment in the 1970s. Most of those programs benefited from a powerful constituency of support. Castaldo needed the state's statutory authorization to bond the accumulated current fund deficit, or he was prepared to request the city council file for bankruptcy. A judge would then have to handle the priorities.

The investment banker for the city of Yonkers recommended hiring me to figure out a bond structure to avoid bankruptcy. When Castaldo and I met, we immediately "bonded." Yet, I had been told by John Connorton, counsel to Governor Carey (and former and later Hawkins partner) that I had to solve the Yonkers fiscal issues without benefitting from all the talent and political pressures being deployed in New York City. Specifically, he told me that creating a municipal assistance corporation for Yonkers could not be legislated that year because Governor Carey was consumed with working with public appointees on the New York City Municipal Assistance Corporation. Those appointees were all highly regarded investment bankers and corporate or nonprofit executives of major New York institutions.

The actual amount of Yonkers's deficit was less than $100 million (compared with New York City's deficit in the billions). So it wasn't a surprise that Yonkers didn't get either the market panic or the press or prominent players that New York City was attracting. Connorton cautioned that, if state legislation authorizing current fund deficit bonding were to be passed, the home rule message requesting passage to be adopted by the city council had to be unanimous. I think he believed obtaining a unanimous council vote in Yonkers was mission impossible!

I also surmised that certain state officials—struggling to solve larger, more public fiscal issues in New York City—would not mind if Yonkers filed for bankruptcy so everyone could learn how the process would work in the state of New York. Specifically, they would discern the priorities among debt service on bonds, funding pension and health pension obligations, and current operating service creditors (including employees, teachers, and those operating the schools).[12]

In the New York "family" of governments, Yonkers seemed like the unplanned child that has a problem fitting in. New York City, Buffalo, Albany, Syracuse, and Rochester are treated as the "big five" mature children, with Yonkers the problem middle child. The smaller so-called cities such as Binghamton, Utica, Lackawanna, and Cohoes were like the favorite youngest children. During the 1975 financial crises of both Yonkers and New York City, Yonkers hardly got any of Albany's attention. It was left to develop its own remedial action to stave off bankruptcy.

Back in my office, I talked with Ike Russell, a seasoned partner who had counseled many New Jersey municipalities to arrange "shot-gun refundings" after the 1929 depression. (This refers to bondholders being forced to exchange longer-term bonds for their existing holdings rather than letting the issuer default on payment of debt service on those holdings.) Russell suggested incorporating the entire New Jersey statutory budget act into a special Yonkers act. It had originally been drafted by Hawkins partners and passed into law in the 1930s as the panacea to permit remarketing of those refunding and new-money municipal bonds in that state. This act referenced *anticipated* revenues against *budgeted* expenditures, each in detail, and mandated a real estate tax increase if a shortfall of revenues resulted.

The Key Power

I did exactly what Russell suggested and added (after reading up on a new auditing recommendation respecting "zero"-based budgeting) filing documents reasonably justifying an increase or decrease from the previous year. To avoid a political battle, the key power to bond the current accumulated general fund deficit was to be based on a number to be certified as correct by an independent accountant. I then inserted a provision for an independent trustee bank to verify that the budget was balanced each year (including such mandated tax, if necessary).

The venerable Arthur Levitt Sr., the longtime routinely elected state comptroller and official charged with issuing state bonds, requested a meeting. With the city council, he wanted to review the proposed act to be presented to the state legislature but before the approval vote of a home rule message. It was a meeting I consider one of my classics.

After I presented the summary of the proposed statute and my thinking about each section, Levitt asked, "Mr. Sigal, what firm are you with?" Upon my answering "Hawkins," he said he knew partners there, particularly Chuck Kades and Frank Wood. He then said I was a fine representative of that firm and that the statute was almost perfect. Then, with controlled anger, he asked why I was turning control of a New York municipality over to a bank. I replied that, of course, I had considered *his* office for that duty. But I thought that, because it involved only a numbers computation and determining reasonable justifications, involving his office could become a political problem. There would undoubtedly follow years of mandated tax increases for which his office could be blamed.

Levitt thanked me and suggested that if Yonkers wanted his support for the legislation, the state comptroller had to be designated as the fiscal agent. The city council then passed the home rule message (unanimously for the first time ever) with the state comptroller as fiscal agent or, with his consent in writing, a bank or trustee company. Years later, Ned Regan, the state's elected comptroller, was subjected to extreme adverse newspaper publicity for permitting a Yonkers budget to be adopted without full compliance with the Budget Act (which would have mandated a tax increase). This underscored my concern about the possible political ramifications, but clearly the policy position of Mr. Levitt was right on.[13]

More on City Manager Vinny Castaldo

Achieving that unanimous vote was even more difficult than expected. At one point in the discussion, Yonkers's city manager became so upset with the maneuvering of Mayor Martinelli, a rare Republican on a mostly Democratic council, he moved the mayor's office from a first-floor ceremonial large office to an enlarged "closet" in the basement for a time.

Another episode between the two occurred on the steps of Yonkers City Hall during a Saturday visit by President Gerald Ford. He was to announce the Model Cities Act, a stepped-up Republican version of federal grants to large cities.[14] The secret service agents had arrived days earlier and had, of course, become buddies with City Manager Vinny Castaldo. He had befriended them with pizza and full cooperation to ensure a safe arrival and departure of the president. A secret service person asked where Vinny would be seated on the podium. Vinny answered, "Because the president is a Republican, the mayor as a Republican sets the protocol and prerogatives on seating placements." The mayor had, of course, made sure Vinny had no place on the platform at all. The secret service agent then suggested Vinny arrange to stand about three rows in front of the podium. When Ford finished speaking and was being escorted out, the agents agreed to spot Vinny, raise the cordon, and introduce him to President Ford.

And that's exactly what happened. The front-page picture in the Yonkers Sunday newspaper showed President Ford shaking hands with Vinny with the bold caption "President Ford congratulates Castaldo on managing well the City." He had arranged for the photographer to be ready and, of course, also told the reporter what Ford had said to him when the photo was taken. The headline was all Vinny.

He told me later that in actuality the only dialogue had been, "Good speech, Mr. President" followed by a "thank you" from the president. That same front page also featured a separate smaller, lower-corner photo of the podium as the President Ford spoke. It showed the mayor straining his neck to be included in a row of relatively unrecognized invitees seated in the back.

Home Rule Message

For the first time in its history, the city council had a unanimous home rule message. Without continuous hearings, the state legislature passed the Yonkers Budget Act, and the bond market (assured of the state comptroller's oversight) bought the ninety-million-dollar bond issue to fund the general fund deficit.

Today, the Yonkers Budget Act continues to be the formal method for budgeting in Yonkers, with its bottom-line mandate forcing a tax increase if reasonable estimates of expenditures exceed reasonable estimates of revenues.

Another Crisis

Yet, this wasn't the last fiscal crisis with an overhanging threat of bankruptcy suffered by Yonkers.[15] On August 3, 1988, Yonkers again was facing a fiscal crisis in failing to enforce a desegregation order. Again, the state under Governor Mario Cuomo was not about to step in to solve the city's financial problem of integrating its schools. In fact, Albany supported the judicial pressure being put on the city council. The federal judge in charge of enforcing the civil rights laws had determined and ordered the payment of increasing numbers of monetary fines by the city if the council refused to adopt the court-ordered desegregation plan. The city manager was quoted as saying, "The city could pay up to $26 million, the cumulative total of the fines, starting at $100 and doubling each day by the eighteenth day." That's when it would run out of money to pay either fines or salaries.

Under the complexity of New York law, Yonkers was liable for the finances of the city's school district, though the school district board was the independent manager of its budget. This represented a typical confusion of New York law between responsibility and liability. Given that the fines would double each period, within a few days the amount would become totally beyond the ability of the tax base to pay. The city would have to file for bankruptcy.

At the time, the bond market had reacted rationally, and the price and ratings of Yonkers bonds were falling to junk status. In my role as bond counsel to the city, I called the city manager on August 4, 1988. We discussed that Judge Sand, despite his current contempt order, needed to recognize that the next judge's court order might require the city to issue bonds for construction of new schools. Therefore, he might consider modifying his order. That would signal to the bond market that the current and timely payment of debt service on outstanding bonds was not at risk.

So, with the knowledge of the city manager, I had our litigation partner document, intervene, and petition the court without having an explicit retainer. The document requested that Judge Sand modify his order and approve funds for the payment of debt service on outstanding bonds. Judge Sand accepted the theory of the petition and ordered the release of funds for debt service. He knew that if he planned to order any kind of remedial action, it would require bonding by the city, and he needed to protect its credit.[16]

Governor Cuomo's counsel, Evan Davis, a good friend of my partner John Connorton, was unhappy with our intervention. Governor Cuomo supported using all methods of pressure on the then-Republican city council to take care of the civil rights issue. However, it wasn't easy to overcome the longstanding residential housing patterns that separated races in Yonkers to provide an integrated schooling policy.

Although the complaint itself was filed in 1980, the case did not actually get settled until 2007. In fact, Judge Sand presided over the case for the entire twenty-seven-year period.

CHAPTER 3

Orange County:
Was It a Municipal Bankruptcy?

This chapter illustrates that the officials of a municipality can be led by counsel to take a course of action that, upon reflection, could be counter to the interests of the taxpayers.

Early in 1995, Hawkins responded to a request for proposals to serve Orange County, California, as bond counsel. It happened during the county's bankruptcy that resulted from excessive leveraging of the multibillion-dollar investments in the Orange County Investment Fund. This fund consisted of pension contributions by the county and its surrounding municipalities[17] and was managed by Robert Citron, who was eventually criminally prosecuted and pleaded guilty to six felony counts. To the end of this life according to the Orange County Register, Citron claimed the County was at fault for declaring bankruptcy, a move he considered ill advised. [18]

On a particular day in late 1994, it was disclosed that the mark-to-market value of the investments in this fund was $12 billion. With the cost of those investments at $14 billion, that meant the fund on the balance sheet was in the red (deficit). Public notice of that "paper loss" caused an immediate demand by panicked municipalities to be

paid out what they had originally deposited.[19] This created an immediate need for cash.

Orange County officials hired a bankruptcy lawyer who immediately filed for bankruptcy for the county. That would make Orange
County the largest municipal bankruptcy in history. Under Chapter 9
of the Federal Bankruptcy Act, a municipality can file for bankruptcy
if it's insolvent, meaning it cannot pay its debt when due. Orange
County proved that it did not have $2,000,000 in the bank and
therefore claimed it could not pay those demanding their money back.
The county hired Salomon Brothers as a financial advisory firm. It
immediately assembled its inside team, including Dale Horowitz, the
managing director of the public finance department and reportedly
the largest stockholder at Salomon, to advise on restructuring debt.
Tom Hayes, former California state treasurer, was also hired to manage
the sale of the pool's investments.

I had worked often with Dale Horowitz and his public finance
department, including as bond counsel for the Alaska Housing
Finance Agency when his firm was the underwriter. I had also been
retained as counsel to his firm in underwriting bond issues for the
Detroit Water and Sewer Revenue Bond issues.

Along with a Cleveland firm, the county had retained Hawkins
as bond counsel, although we were expected to work *with* but not
for the bankruptcy counsel. We were asked to delve into the financial
documentation and assist the bankruptcy counsel and financial
advisor in their efforts to either:

- Challenge the propriety of the underwritings of each of the
  prior transactions, or
- Provide legal analysis on a potential refunding of those leveraged
  bond issues.

Our retainer also included reviewing other options than continuing
in bankruptcy. That might include cooperating with previous or new

underwriters to raise the cash to pay off the claimants. However, the bankruptcy counsel had already determined a litigation strategy to sell the below-market investments as soon as possible before further market deterioration. Doing this would establish the pension fund loss. That loss would be recovered from the proceeds of litigation and settlement negotiation with the investment bankers who allegedly had improperly provided the excess leveraging advice!

On my plane flight to California, I read the most recent offering document put out by Orange County for its routine general obligation bond sale. I learned Orange County was, with Westchester County, New York (a longstanding Hawkins client), among the richest counties in the nation. It was then and still is a rock-ribbed, Ronald Reagan Republican county with expensive homes and a robust economy of mixed and profitable businesses. I surmised Orange County had the creditworthiness to issue $2 billion in bonds to pay off the claimants and then, over time if needed, to liquidate the portfolio.[20] The security of the bond issue would be the general obligation of the county.

My New England upbringing had me at first thinking that these Orange County officials would be embarrassed to be in bankruptcy; they'd want to get out of it as quickly and prudently as possible. So my first question to Bruce Bennett, the bankruptcy attorney, was, "How much is needed to pay out all the claimants?" He replied, "About two billion dollars." I told him that amount might be doable, but I should have been more sensitive as I said it. I was thinking the county could issue that amount of its general obligation bonds to pay the claimants. The bankruptcy counsel was determined to pursue a litigation strategy establish from the sale of the securities and allege losses and collect from the investment banks. He had been retained before me, and the alleged abusive leveraging was already well documented. This was the first time I had heard that those bankers were "enablers," encouraging Mr. Citron to unwisely leverage his portfolio that was "under water."

Presented Offer

I made a call to Eric Altman, a close investment banking friend at
J. P. Morgan, who agreed to research and, if feasible, present a proposal
to underwrite a $2 billion general obligation bond issue. Three weeks
later, he flew out to present that option to the board. The bankruptcy
attorney refused to let him in the room, citing confidentiality. At that
point, I was called on to convey the essence of the offer. We were
seated in front of the board members with Bennett on the left,
Horowitz in the center, and me on the right.

Horowitz and I had been joined at the hip during the New York
City fiscal crisis. There, our firms cooperated in bonding out the
accrued general fund liability of New York City to avoid bankruptcy.
Because we had seen eye to eye at that time, it did not occur to me
to have a heads-up discussion with him before the meeting about
the J. P. Morgan proposal. Frankly, even if it had occurred to me, I
probably would not have considered it proper to try to sway his view
because I expected J. P. Morgan to make the proposal with all three
of us hearing it for the first time. In fact, I expected he would readily
agree it was the best way to reestablish the marketability of Orange
County bonds and restore its credit rating, especially because of our
all-out efforts to keep New York City from filing for bankruptcy.

Bennett argued that cramming down (a court's involuntary
imposition of a reorganization plan despite objections of some creditors) on the holders of the leveraged bonds and suing and collecting
damages from the underwriters of those bonds would be the best way
of recovering the loss. He also said that issuing new bonds at this
time would be counterproductive and preclude his ability to claim
damages in his lawsuits against the investment bankers. Finally, it
came down to Horowitz's thoughts. He shocked me as I recall that
he threw up his hands and said, "I'm sitting between two extremely

capable lawyers. We have a judgment call to be made by the board and not to be made by a financial advisor. Each position has merit." Board members seemed surprised and apparently had never realized they had an option other than bankruptcy. Already, they'd been briefed by Bennett that his approach for collecting damages by suing the underwriters would be successful. Thus, the board stuck with Bennett.

Hawkins and our co-bond counsel Cleveland firm were fired two weeks later, replaced by a New York corporate firm with a large bankruptcy practice and small public finance group.[21] I was then warned in a telephone call by Bennett that if I or any of my Hawkins partners publicly disclosed why we were replaced, we would be sued for breach of the confidential client privilege. Why? Because, I surmised, the J. P. Morgan proposal was reasonable and doable in mitigating the damages, and it would hamper his "litigate everybody, everywhere" strategy.

Two takeaways: First, I did not appreciate in that meeting that Salomon was conflicted as a financial advisor on the J. P. Morgan restructured bond issue option because the firm, with its affiliate Tom Hayes, was allegedly making substantial commissions from the sale of the securities invested in the pool. They would be selling the securities fast to establish the losses needed in litigation by Bennett to establish the amount of damages with which to claim reimbursement from the underwriters. Horowitz probably never appreciated such an apparent conflict or even bothered to assess whether it was the right financial strategy to immediately sell those securities, since Salomon, in defense, I presume, could claim, if challenged, it was acting on the instruction of the county's bankruptcy counsel.

Second, here are the facts (established in hindsight): By liquidating the investment pool in 1994, Orange County locked in a loss of $1.6 billion. It would have been wise to hold those investments for a month, because the market price came back to their original purchase prices. If they had been held for three to four months, the pricing would have been triple the purchase price. Furthermore, and most important, the cash to be received from the maturity in the normal course of the original investments was scheduled properly to pay what participants needed to pay their pension obligations. In other words, the mark-to-market pricing did not reflect the prudent manner in which Citron had planned the investments, nor did it reflect the proper market analysis of the securities in that investment pool. In fact, none of those securities were defaulting. It was only that the interest being paid was not as high as market index rates at the time. The whole fiasco was based on a misunderstanding of "mark to market." It also hinged on the haste of the bankruptcy attorney to resist an alternate, reasonable restructuring solution and the financial advisor to not appreciate the apparent conflict of interest as both advisor to the seller of those securities and advisor on market options for county bonding.[22]

Noteworthy is that later, a similar fund comprising a pool of investments in bonds suffered a similar mark-to-market loss.[23] With huge losses and trading on its shares halted, MF Global, managed by former New Jersey Governor Jon Corzine, declared bankruptcy. Reportedly, this made MF Global one of the biggest bankruptcies in U.S. history. However, in that bankruptcy, the trustee administering the fund did not make the same decision (mistake) of immediately selling or in fact ever selling the investments in the sovereign securities in that portfolio. Instead, the trustee recognized that "mark to market" was not a stigma on the quality of the investments.

Over time, the securities recovered in full their market price. As a result, all investments were returned to the investors—called a "hodgepodge of farmers, smalltime investors and hedge funds." They received a 100 percent return of their investment within two years of filing, losing only interest during that period.[24]

Two lessons learned from the Orange County and MF Global Bankruptcies are:

- There should be certain restrictions on withdrawal of funds by investors in a pooled investment fund, and

- Mark-to-market valuation is not by itself the proper criteria with which to appreciate the value of investments in an investment pool.

Basic Defect in Bankruptcy Strategy

A third point the Orange County case illustrates is that of a basic defect in Chapter 9 of the Federal Bankruptcy Statute (discussed in Chapter 5). The test of insolvency—not having cash to pay debts when they're due—may work well enough for corporations; these owners are naturally motivated to borrow to avoid filing for bankruptcy. But this test is the wrong one for municipalities. Why? Because that test does not consider whether or not the municipality can borrow through a bank loan or a bond issue to raise the cash to pay its debts when due. There was no financial doubt that Orange County had market access based on its general obligation credit, so its filing was a political/business choice, not a necessity.

In theory, the basic asset of any state or municipality is its willingness to pay its debts when due. But in today's climate, the concept of issuing debt to restructure indebtedness coming due (thereby showing a willingness) has been compromised by the defect in Chapter 9 of the Federal Bankruptcy Act. It provides a politically easy way out for an executive to claim an inability to pay outstanding bonded debt (as has happened in Detroit and in Puerto Rico, discussed in the chapters that follow).

CHAPTER 4

Detroit and Puerto Rico:
Bankruptcy in Play

*This chapter reflects on whether a better recovery option
could have been selected for the government entities discussed here. If the answer is yes, is there a practical or
legal way of protecting critical stakeholders consisting of
employees, bondholders, taxpayers, and service creditors
so a better option would have surfaced?*

Every fiscal crisis has several variables. However, in each case, the
government entity has assets, taxing power, borrowing power,
employees with embedded health and pension benefits, bondholders
with various securities and priorities, and other creditors providing
services.

Orange County is a rich, robust county whose officials made a
business decision to stay in bankruptcy not with standing it could
market its own general-obligation bonds to get the resources to pay
other government investors in its leveraged retirement fund. Unfortunately, the business decision was based on advice that failed to analyze
the portfolio of investments in the pool as maturing as required for
scheduled payouts to pensioners. Decision makers misinterpreted
the mark-to-market valuation as an indication of the poor quality

of those investments. The result was an unnecessary panic of pool investors. Hence, losses and litigation followed, rather than a $2 billion profit. As indicated in Chapter 3, in the case of MF Global, the trustee smartly held that pool of investments, learning from the Orange County mistake.

Bankruptcy Is Almost Always the Wrong Option

I strongly suggest that insolvency proceedings for a state or bankruptcy under Chapter 9 of the Federal Bankruptcy Act for a municipality is almost always the wrong option. At the outset of this nation, the fiscal principle for government demanded by Alexander Hamilton was to pay at full value and honor the pledge of faith and credit. This means no discounting of the amount that one is contractually obligated to pay.

More important, factors that apply to corporate debt and corporate bankruptcy do not necessarily carry over to state and municipal debt. In my view, corporate bankruptcy lawyers and financial advisors do not get that message. It is a basic mistake for state and municipal leaders to retain corporate rather than municipal consultants at the outset of a fiscal crisis.

The Treasury Asset Relief Program or TARP was created to restructure debt of private corporations using federal loans. TARP was applied in the bankruptcy cases of General Motors and Chrysler. TARP, in those corporate bailouts, was the starting point of the shoddy treatment of bondholders. How? TARP prioritized employee pension and health benefits owned by employees, disregarding the bond preferences or parity for classes of other creditors. This became the precedent for similar preferential treatment for employee pension and health benefits and the haircutting of bondholders in Detroit and Puerto Rico. President Barack Obama himself labeled the Chrysler bondholders "speculators," an obvious derogatory remark, and publicly supported their shoddy treatment.[25]

The repudiation of bonded debt as occurred in the Chrysler TARP corporate bankruptcy goes against the Hamiltonian principles as they apply to governmental debt. The Obama administration could properly justify its approach of shedding bond debt in a *corporate* bankruptcy by speculating that Chrysler would regain solvency by selling cars. At the same time, the policy would protect employees and be accepted as legitimate public policy to keep the automobile industry in the U.S.

Yet, it seems obvious that the Obama administration failed to appreciate basic differences between corporate and governmental debt when it came to the bankruptcy of the city of Detroit. First, the city of Detroit does not make cars or any other product, and its taxpayer base is not moving to Mexico. Its basic asset is its willingness to pay its debt—its "pledge of its faith and credit" to those bondholders who provided the cash to build infrastructure and sometimes balance budgets by funding deficits during recessions.

Second, the taxpayers in Detroit were the most important stakeholders in a municipal bankruptcy. Yet, they were not represented in the proceedings, especially as their elected officials were sidelined and labeled the "culprits" who caused the fiscal crisis by issuing allegedly excessive debt. Its underwriting investment bankers and insurers of that debt were labeled "enablers" by lending to that issuer without doing "due diligence" on that issuer's ability to repay. Both issuer and bondholders became the problem as perpetrators of excessive debt.

The Case of Detroit

Let's discuss Detroit's situation, which was summarized in a *Washington Post* article published in 2017.[26]

In representing states, cities, and municipalities, I have always looked for the basic asset or wealth of an issuer. For instance, Connecticut—with its high-income residents in Fairfield County and the towns surrounding Hartford, Bridgeport, and New Haven —has the highest income per resident except for Alaska. (Alaska's income tends to be high to attract workers to that remote state and because of high transportation costs to deliver goods.)

New York City features tourists being attracted to its theaters, major museums, and fantastic apartments. That lures the wealthy people from Japan, China, and Russia to an exciting city and a safe haven from any regime change at home. California has a coastline and beautiful beaches second to none as well as the movie industry in Los Angeles and the sophisticated ambiance of San Francisco.

What can be said about Detroit? It had automobile manufacturing, a regional industry perhaps returning to prosperity, a water supply system, and other infrastructure components built to last for centuries. It has a vibrant professional sports industry with the Detroit Tigers, Lions, Red Wings, and Pistons. The city owned outright a world-class art collection worth billions on the open market. Given that most art collections are owned by nonprofit entities, no other city in America owned such an assessible and recognized asset.

But it had become clear that the city of Detroit had been mismanaged to the point that its bond debt and obligations to employees for retirement and health benefits had become too much to pay at current schedules. It also couldn't balance its budget without making tax increases that would be too high for taxpayers or reducing expenses at current service levels. Those factors were also in play in Philadelphia, Scranton, New York City, Yonkers, Bridgeport, Waterbury, and several Rhode Island communities.

Proposed Bankruptcy for Detroit

The option for Detroit to seek bankruptcy initiated by Governor Richard Snyder was no doubt influenced by the state's choice of consultants, both legal and financial. Those consultants proposed bankruptcy for Detroit because they were primarily corporate-oriented litigation professionals inclined against or even unappreciative of the sobriety of cooperative state and municipal restructuring. That would involve reaching a consensus with bondholders, unions, and insurers to preserve the honor of the issuer.

Moreover, the Jones Day bankruptcy lawyers retained by the governor even argued and convinced the federal judge involved that negotiations with creditors (a legal first precondition in a bankruptcy proceeding under Chapter 9) was an impractical waste of time. Those lawyers argued the technicality that, in bankruptcy, the assets of a municipal issuer were not available for sale. But that fact proved to be an empty shibboleth, as gifts of assets to the insurers ended the bankruptcy. Clearly, an appraisal of the city's assets would have proven that leveraging those assets—including the art collection if properly evaluated and monetized—would have been sufficient to restructure and secure refunding debt with much longer maturities. One commentator said, "Selling the collection isn't even necessary. Money is lent against art all the time."[27] But some corporate bankruptcy lawyers advising municipalities that are in fiscal stress are simply not familiar with (or, in my opinion, choose to conceal) the many ways and means of restructuring, refunding, and exchanging municipal debt as well as creating new security for additional bonds for new projects. That is the essence of self-sufficiency for municipalities.

The irony here is that the Detroit restructured bonds could have matured to well over fifty years because the basic asset available, the art, has a period of probable usefulness ("ppu") of well in excess of one hundred years. And artwork does not depreciate like a building or a bridge. A loan-to-value analysis of the collection at 50% would have yielded a half-billion dollars—easily enough money to solve the deficit issue.[28] In public finance parlance, the maturity of the bonds is parallel with the "ppu" for arbitrage and security purposes.

In fact, from when Governor Snyder first made the call to his New York corporate financial consultant friend from New York and early on listened only to the Jones Day spiel, the city of Detroit was on the bankruptcy track. Any principles of "willingness to pay," restructuring of debt, or preserving self-sufficiency were not publicized and probably, in my opinion, even considered. "Bankruptcy on a fast track timeline" became Snyder's motto. Bring in the Jones Day partner as overseer to manage the message, and the rest is history.

A Hamiltonian Solution

What would Hamilton have done to preserve the creditworthiness of Detroit? I suggest he would have convened a meeting with the governor, the mayor, the bondholders' committee (including the bond insurers), the union leaders, the secretary of the Treasury, and a taxpayer coalition he would have created. First, he would have made it clear that no one (even he) was suggesting the art collection be sold.

Second, he would have taught the great universities and hospitals successfully market tax-exempt bonds by attracting investors to bond issuances secured by a first mortgage on the hospital buildings and/or the university facilities. I believe Hamilton would have made clear that no investor of those bonds is expecting to dismantle or sell those facilities by foreclosing on that mortgage security. He would have structured a refunding transaction secured by the art collection. It would have included a safeguard provision precluding any remedy that would have included a sale of the collection (except in the ordinary course of prudent art portfolio management) in the unlikely event the city defaulted on paying the restructured debt secured by the mortgage on the collection. The new bonds so secured would be issued with long maturities at favorable rates. Favorable rates would have been achieved because the insurance companies insuring out-standing bonds would have insured the new issue rather than write the checks on the outstanding insured bonds. Holders of the uninsured outstanding bonds would exchange their bonds for the new bonds rather than having to write off and incur haircuts of the principal, as actually happened. (The exchange transaction was exactly the solution devised by many municipalities in New Jersey in 1930s and are referenced as "shotgun refundings.")

Additional bonds could have been secured by other of the various revenues generated by the city's assets. They would include privatization of facilities at the airport owned by the city, the toll bridge to Canada, a percentage of parking revenues from the garage at the bridge, sales tax on spectator tickets at various sports venues, and other city assets that were eventually given to bondholders in the settlement of this case.

Hamilton may have even insisted on better relationships between the city as owner of its water and sewer system and the outlying communities as contractees, but he would not have forced the regional consolidation or trashed the security of the Detroit sewer and water revenue bonds. To summarize, he would have honored the "faith and credit pledge" of the city to pay its general obligation bonds and respected, as valid, the pledged seniority of the city's revenue bonds. He knew that market credibility is key to a future Detroit's ability to access the bond market and stand on its own credits.

The Grand Bargain (The Grand Theft)

But the city of Detroit's taxpayers, employees, and bondholders lost. Unfortunately, the federal judge went along with the governor's lawyers to prevent a solution that Hamilton would have favored. In an obvious irony, the gift of the art collection to a nonprofit organization for about 10 percent of its value was called the Grand Bargain. This deal became the cornerstone of the judge's hubris in thinking this solution was best for the city's taxpayers.

Again, I say the art collection could have been mortgaged as security to restructure the outstanding debt over a long maturation period by applying the public finance precedents available from university and hospital tax-exempt bond structures. This approach was considered but, in my view, not seriously as no proposals were requested. The publicized concern was that if the restructured debt could not be repaid, then the art collection would have to be liquidated. Still, can you imagine any private corporation being allowed to give away its major asset in a bankruptcy before providing payment to its stockholders?

In this way, the taxpayers of Detroit were deprived of monetizing any of its major asset and thereby preserving its self-sufficiency and creditworthiness as well as honoring its pledge of faith and credit. The opportunity was lost to come before or out of bankruptcy with a refunding bond issue secured by any of the city's assets. Unlike Chrysler, the city has no product to sell; its only other asset—its faith and credit—had been severely damaged.

Treatment of Bond Insurers

The treatment of the bond insurers was also interesting, because they were "given" valuable assets of the city in exchange for accepting the losses resulting from the payment on the insured bonds. This compromise was approved by the bankruptcy judge who had originally ruled that negotiations with creditors was impractical. The toll bridge to Windsor, parking garages, and Joe Louis Arena were deeded over; so was a substantial amount of land the city held in foreclosure. Thus, these creditors become sole-source investors in city assets. No public bidding was offered, so who knew what other entrepreneurs would have paid or what innovative proposals Detroit may have received?

Without any legal proceeding adjudicating the issue, the federal judge even went so far as declaring void certain bonds known as Certificates of Participation. He ruled that those obligations be paid at about 10 cents on the dollar—a 90 percent haircut—while the entire proceeds of those bonds remained in the investment trust of the pension funds. In my opinion, a more dishonorable result of unjust enrichment cannot be envisioned, and yet the federal judge allowed that to happen. Overall, "faith and credit" principles embedded in public finance precedents were undermined by these parties: the bankruptcy court; the Republican governor of Michigan; corporate financial and legal bankruptcy consultants; and the then Democratic mayor of Detroit.

The Story of Puerto Rico[29]

The Puerto Rico fiscal crisis began with the public announcement by Governor Alejandro García Padilla of Puerto Rico that the Commonwealth could not pay its $72 billion of bonded debt. Padilla had hired the international law firm of Cleary Gottlieb and clearly was adhering to the plan of that counsel. Yet the fact of hiring that firm was never disclosed by the Government Development Bank to the underwriters working on a $3 billion new offering. (That plan is described in explicit detail in a five-hundred dollar priced book on a sovereign repudiation of debt process written by partners at Cleary Gottlieb as the model strategy for sovereign nations willing to shirk the obligation to pay debt.[30])

Sovereign nations that create such a fiscal crisis and repudiate their debt obligations are known as "banana republics." According to the plan, these leaders soften up the bond creditors by declaring an inability to pay the country's debt, thereby destroying the bond market value by anywhere from 90 to 25 cents. That then triggers hedge funds to buy out the original, good-faith investors at a deep discount. They keep the pressure of publicity of nonpayment going until the price on the bonds sinks lower. Then such a sovereign nation seeks to pay off the bonds at the depressed priced by issuing new bonds.

When the governor announced on June 28, 2015, that Puerto Rico could not pay its $72 billion in bonded debt,[31] the public finance community appeared to react without objection or perhaps even with relief. One municipal financial advisor told me that Puerto Rico had betrayed the bond market by routinely promising budget reform and never following through because the government repeatedly borrowed to cover operating deficits.

Unlike in 2006, no firm from public finance was asked to submit a plan to restructure the debt, because the governor had put the Cleary playbook into play. Later on, public finance professionals, including the insurers of Puerto Rico bonds, realized what was happening. By that time, the Cleary play was only at intermission, but clearly no restructuring of debt would happen without serious haircuts in some form of an insolvency process.

Puerto Rico is not a sovereign nation. It was then considered a Commonwealth governed by its own constitution and the federal constitution, including the contract non-impairment clause. Because of that, the next step was to appeal for relief to President Obama and the U.S. Congress. Like U.S. states, filing for bankruptcy under the current federal bankruptcy law was not a legal option. In fact, the proper forum for resolving its fiscal crisis was open to debate, but not for long.

The U.S. Treasury became the leading advocate for returning Puerto Rico to a territory under the direct oversight of the federal government by a board appointed by the POTUS (president of the United States) and Congress. The priorities of debt established under Puerto Rico's constitution would no longer be the law. A new law, known as PROMESA, passed and was signed by President Obama. By doing so, I believe PROMESA trashed the Hamiltonian principles of honoring bonded debt. Ironically, the signing happened on the same day the actors in the Broadway play *Hamilton* were being honored at the White House.

The PROMESA board was not mandated to follow either the state debt or federal contract constitutional provisions; rather, it was empowered to resolve the fiscal crisis as its members thought fair.

Moreover, unlike the Chrysler crisis in which the federal government advanced interim funds to keep production going, no interim lending was included in the PROMESA legislation. It became the irony of all ironies that Puerto Rico's newly elected Governor Ricky Rosselló had indicated his willingness to negotiate a restructuring with off-island bondholders and insurers before the election and was well briefed by me in a short New York meeting in my office building that his first budget could include an island-wide property tax to secure those restructured bonds. But he turned against those creditors. In effect, he put nothing in his budget for such debt service, and never put the option of such a tax on the table.

Why did that happen?

Now that Rosselló has resigned amid the disclosure of his emails about his despicable attitude toward his constituency, it has become clear to me, in my opinion, that he and his inner circle were intent on preventing an island wide tax on private property. Despite several emails requesting a meeting. Neither he or his assistant invited me to discuss or fully develop such a proposal.

Maybe he realized the damage done to the Commonwealth's rule of law by PROMESA was permanent. The island would not get back to the market alone; it would stay as a territory of the U.S. and be completely dependent on the U.S. Treasury guaranteeing its debt. Therefore, why pay any existing bondholder or the insurance companies? And more important, why advocate for levying a property tax for that purpose?

The PROMESA board and the governor agreed to cover all obligations to other creditors and to employees, including pension and health benefits. The governor even supported full payment to the holders of bonds who are residents of Puerto Rico[32] on the theory that the Government Development Bank encouraged those holders to buy the bonds as badges of loyalty—like war bonds.

Shady Plan

To repeat: Governor Padilla's statement about an inability to pay Puerto Rico's debt was the first salvo in a disguised plan (promoted by the large corporate law firm counseling the governor) to trash, as detailed in that $500 book, and thus reduces the market price of the island's bonded indebtedness. That would provide the Commonwealth with the opportunity to work an exchange or refund its debt at the reduced market price (in effect, a repudiation of the willingness to pay the face value of the bonds). This is much like what the "banana republics" of South America do, including the government of Argentina, another client of that corporate law firm. The entire debauchery of debt management practiced by sovereigns came into play in Puerto Rico and shaded the rest of the actions of the Padilla administration.

The financial report, prepared by a consultant (an expert in sovereign debt only and retained by the Cleary firm), bolstered Puerto Rico's "inability to pay." The report dismissed the statutory power to tax real and personal property as irrelevant because it supposedly needed updated appraisals. Outdated appraisals can be used so long as appraisals of all property are equally outdated, as they only affect the rates. Thus, the basic core of general obligation contracted debt—using full taxing power—was, in my analysis, purposely ignored eliminated as an option. Even an investment banking firm proposing a special corporate income tax to replicate the securitization of COFINA was also eliminated as an option. The owners of hotels, casinos, golf courses, beachfront condos, and vast amounts of land owned by private interests awaiting development escaped a special recovery corporate income or property tax. Either revenue resource could have secured a refunding issue that would have restructured the outstanding debt with longer maturities and, coupled with proper PROMESA budget oversight, saved millions of fees and permitted Puerto Rico to regain market access by this time.

In summary, honoring the contract implicit in the "faith and credit pledge," the core principle of governmental credit (as preached by Hamilton) was completely trashed by the U.S. Treasury under President Obama and the U.S. Congress. In accordance with the federally enacted statute, the Commonwealth of Puerto Rico was returned to a territory controlled by the U.S. government. This totally subrogated the adopted constitution approved by the citizens of Puerto Rico *and* shut down the bond market to the territory. In effect, any new capital financing would have to carry the guarantee of the federal government. Undoubtedly, several of the revenue-generating infrastructures (such as the utilities) will be privatized. Why President Obama and Congress did not follow the federal legislative precedent of imposing oversight of the District of Columbia and restructuring its debt remains a mystery.

In trying to protect their holdings, bond market participants have sued and countersued each other for priority of payment. Yet they failed to cooperate in logically analyzing the law and the assets available. Hence, the COFINA bondholders were pledged the revenues from the sales tax adopted in 2006. (In effect, this followed a legislative precedent adopted by New York State to remedy the New York City fiscal crisis in 1975. See Chapter 1 reflecting the adoption of law upheld by the highest court of the state of New York.)

It was not until the fiscal crisis that the general obligation holders were challenging that securitization, claiming those revenues are required by Puerto Rico's constitution to pay its bonds.[33] So from 2006 to 2018, general obligation bonds were issued, marketed, and remarketed along with COFINA bond issues aggregating $15 billion. Also (and to emphasize again), those general obligation bondholders have the statutory legal power to require the government to exercise its taxing power and implement an island-wide tax without limitation as to rate or amount on all real and personal taxable property. The enabling taxing statute is law. It had been implemented and levied to a limited extent in earlier budgets and has the proper public policy exceptions for the poor and elderly. Yet no groundswell supporting its imposition is evident. It is natural that the resorts, casinos, and wealthy property owners have not suggested such exercise of taxing power, but the question remains, *why haven't those in charge levied taxes?* Perhaps implementing it is such a hot potato, force of the politically powerful has silenced any advocate.

I made a sustained effort to present such an option to the U.S. Treasury as a way Puerto Rico could restructure its debt and honor its full faith and credit pledge. However, it was dismissed as "old school"—the term used by the third-ranking official of the U.S. Treasury, Kent Hiteshew. I understand that an investment banker proposed a corporate tax securitization as a restructuring option, but that too was ignored. Again, what is shocking is that those Treasury officials chose to overlook the relatively recent legislation passed by Congress in respect to the District of Columbia fiscal crisis. It was modeled after the New York legislation and successfully implemented to restore the District's bond market credit.

Before becoming a Treasury official, Hiteshew was an experienced officer in the municipal finance department of J. P. Morgan. He was well versed in restructuring municipal bonds and securitizing municipal revenues. Clearly, a deal had been reached.[34] Despite repeated efforts to focus him on the available precedents of public finance to stymie insolvency, he chose to climb on board with the corporate-oriented department officials.

To repeat: the PROMESA Act explicitly returned that island to a territory under rule of Congress and neutered the force of any provision of law in the Commonwealth's constitution. Hence, as a

Commonwealth Constitutional law issue, the controversy became moot between general obligation bondholders and COFINA, a corporation owned and controlled by the Puerto Rican government with bonds payable from and secured by a first lien on the island's sales tax. A judge ruled that the priority of claims under the Commonwealth constitution is not relevant; the issue must be decided under the PROMESA federal statute.[35] The reasoning? If the oversight board need not abide the provisions of that Constitution, then what is the point of referring the issue to a Commonwealth court?

The COFINA senior debtholders and the general obligation holders made a deal that gave each a secured interest in the sales tax revenues. The key to their deal was debt restructuring and exchange of both the general obligation and COFINA bonds for new bonds approved by the PROMESA board. My understanding is that the bonds accepted in exchange (and the security provisions thereof) enjoy contract protection under the federal Constitution. In this way, it precludes these new bonds from creating a repeat of the nullification of the rule of law by amendments to PROMESA.[36] This deal is discussed in detail in the next chapter.

Fiscal Crises of the City of Detroit and the Commonwealth of Puerto Rico

Hamilton's respect for full debt payment starts from the fact that the dollar constitutes a contract for the payment of which the "faith and credit" of the United States is pledged. Under the U.S. Constitution, Congress cannot pass any laws that impair contracts unless compensation is paid or, with respect to municipal debt instruments, unless the provisions respecting municipal governments (such as Chapter 9 of the Bankruptcy Law) are followed.

To summarize, the Federal Bankruptcy Act does not apply to any state of the United States or to Puerto Rico, Guam, Virgin Islands, American Samoa, or Northern Mariana Islands. Hence, regarding

Puerto Rico, the Obama administration led the charge to return the Commonwealth to the status of a territory, so it could then impose an oversight board and provide a bankruptcy process. That legislation explicitly provided that the priorities on payment of debtholders and creditors (established in the voter-approved constitution of Puerto Rico) need not be followed. The oversight board has a "fairness" standard to apply those issues. That means by returning the island to the legal status of a territory, the rule of state law was abandoned. As a result, it left questions of impairment of contract, due process, and perhaps other protections to the federal constitution.

Naturally, the litigators, lobbyists, and financial consultants descended on the island. It will be years before basic rights of U.S. citizen-taxpayers in Puerto Rico will be restored.[37] The officials of the U.S. Treasury and/or President Obama knowingly abandoned the Hamiltonian principles. It seems many precedents of resolving governmental fiscal crisis by consensus of the creditors were deemed "old school."

Detroit and Puerto Rico: Comparisons

In both Detroit and Puerto Rico, Hamilton's basic principle of a willingness to pay debt at par value and to honor a "faith and credit pledge" was scuttled in favor of repudiation or discounting. This resulted in a loss of independence—in Detroit as a governing city and in Puerto Rico as a commonwealth. The fact that Detroit will be the ward of the state of Michigan and Puerto Rico the ward of the United States for perhaps the rest of this century is a given. Why? Because each has lost access to the bond market without state (for Detroit) or federal (for Puerto Rico) enhancement. Yet these results could have been avoided if the leaders had recognized the actual assets or values and then sought to honor their debt obligations rather than repudiate debt.

In these cases, the time-honored twentieth-century examples of restructuring governmental debt were simply ignored. The corporate approach of cramming down on debtholders seemed enticing, especially as venture capitalists began buying up the bonds at well below market value. This left only bond insurers with massive reserves to take the losses.

The perversion of this approach brought to the fore the bankruptcy/litigation law firms representing the deep pocket hedge funds who then faced off against similar big corporate bankruptcy/litigation law firms representing Detroit or Puerto Rico or the insurer or the unions. Litigation everywhere for priority of payments became the primary focus. How different from the fiscal crises in New York City, Bridgeport, the District of Columbia, or Philadelphia where any degenerate behavior was censored by the cooperative efforts of public finance firms and all creditors to restructure debt.

Moreover, the public finance bond market professionals failed the taxpayers of Detroit and Puerto Rico by not waging an all-out campaign to establish that those bond issues benefited the issuer because they were used to build infrastructure or carry the issuer over bad economic periods. They were underwritten in good faith reliance of the issuers' willingness to pay and on explicit representations of city and GDB officials' respecting budget reform and the essential need or public purpose of the financings. The public finance professionals such as bond counsel and financial advisors were silent. They feared lawsuits or even gamed the crisis by accepting supplicant retainers from corporate bankruptcy litigation law firms retained on any side —service creditors, employees, bondholders, the state, the city, the territory, and so on.

No one was retained to represent the taxpayers.

Note: In Appendix A, you'll find my memorandum to the state treasurer outlining the cooperative, consensus approach suggested in this chapter. I had met State Treasurer Andy Dillon at regular conferences of the National Association of State Treasurers and discussed the consensus approach based on my New York and Connecticut retainers. He was persuaded that my approach was not only honorable but doable. He finally said he would provide me with a meeting to make my pitch directly to Michigan Governor Rick Snyder. Unfortunately, the night after that, he beat up his wife and soon there after resigned.[38] Thus, his promise of letting me outline *my* plan to the governor fell by the wayside.

Detroit's Future

What can be said about Detroit? Is the drama over, or is there a lurking law that can be rediscovered and applied?

I suggest the city's taxpayers could revisit the so-called Grand Bargain and identify the transaction by its true name—the Grand Theft. In the law relative to the facts, counsel for the taxpayers could reference all actions involved in the heist as null and void because its sale to the nonprofit at a deeply discounted price constitutes an "adhesion"[39] contract. It could be so ruled by a fair-minded judge and judicially voided as lacking the authorization of the taxpayers, being against public policy, and having been bulldozed through by the proponents without due process.

No bankruptcy law could possibly have anticipated such a deeply discounted giveaway of *the* asset of the bankrupt municipality—what the law calls "ultra vires." Certainly, it can be called a Fifth Amendment "taking" without fair compensation.

Perhaps the taxpayers can achieve compensation for its true value from the primary perpetrators of the fraud—the federal government and the state of Michigan—akin to compensations made to Indian tribes for taking of tribal land. In other words, they could litigate and then negotiate to leave the art collection with the nonprofit but provide taxpayers with federal and state compensation to cover its 90% loss. This option avoids a forced return of the art asset.

There were many behind-the-scenes scenarios before and after the bankruptcy that did not allow advice from those who could have offered standard methods of monetizing the art. With proper investigation in my opinion, the Grand Bargain might be proven to be a fraudulent transfer.[40]

Someone should lift the blinds on this shady deal.

More on Steven W. Rhodes, the Federal Bankruptcy Judge

After the completion of the bankruptcy, the federal judge and others went "on the road" as conference speakers to brag about their heroic efforts in saving the city of Detroit. Those engagements lasted one month, as it became clear that many professionals (including me) in the bond market considered the story a complete sham, calling it a shameful episode in the history of public finance.[41] Many public finance professionals value the teachings of consensus restructuring from New York City in 1975 and the successful marketing of a bond issue restructuring outstanding debt secured by a municipal asset. But that lesson was lost in transition by those who perceived that the art collection should not be put at risk, if nominal, and to preserve the pledge of the good faith and credit of Detroit. And, yes, selling it to a nonprofit for ten cents on the dollar (a "Grand Theft") kept the collection intact for viewing in that region. But the collection would have also been available for such viewing if it had been leveraged in a debt restructuring.

CHAPTER 5

Detroit and Puerto Rico:
Current Status

Since the preceding chapter was first written in the fall of 2018, fiscal facts in both Detroit and Puerto Rico have evolved. In fact, they confirm my point that the outcomes in both bankruptcies have greatly benefited consultants. However, they have not reopened the bond market or created a viable bond structure for the ongoing capital infrastructure needs for either.

Detroit's Situation in 2019

In December 2018, Detroit issued $135,000,000 of standalone general obligation bonds backed by its full "faith and credit pledge" and two percentage points above average triple A rates. The financial pundits did not consider the rate much of a penalty for having filed for bankruptcy. However, the small size of the issue suggests this offering doesn't provide a benchmark for any serious market reception of any sizeable amount of general obligation Detroit bonds in the future.

The so-called security documentation for this general obligation issue even had to include daily escrowing of taxes equal to the accruing debt service on the bonds. I consider this a cosmetic pledge since it creates no priority over the other creditors in bankruptcy. In addition, the offering statement claims a "timely action in the nature of a mandamus" (a judicial writ), implying that certification and collection of adequate taxes is available. But again, that doesn't create any bond security preference for those taxes in a bankruptcy. The offering statement warned that there can be no assurance these taxes will be treated as special revenues (the Chapter 9 term related to treatment of priority for bonds) in a subsequent bankruptcy for the city.

The bottom line is this: The city of Detroit has not emerged with any long-term bond structure of market value. Many market experts agree, the size of this first general obligation issue is too small for anyone to claim a successful bond market reopening.

Compare this "solution" to the New York City's emergence from its 1975 fiscal crisis with several viable multibillion-dollar market-based borrowings that recognized success in emerging from a fiscal crisis. The bond structures that have stood the test of public marketing for the past fifty years are the Municipal Assistance Corporation, the Transitional Finance Authority, the New York City Water Authority, and various tax increment funding structures, as well as New York City's standard general obligation bonds. The innovative financing structures were challenged based on constitutional issues. Those structures were fully litigated and validated by approving opinions of the Court of Appeals, New York State's highest court. That process and those precedents gave the rating agencies the basis for high ratings because of the security pledge and no litigation risk.

Unfortunately, this kind of validation of a market-accepted bonding structure for future capital infrastructure borrowings did not happen in Detroit or in Puerto Rico.

In my analysis, the bankruptcy failure in Detroit and in Puerto Rico is attributable to a basic lack of understanding of public finance and marketing municipal bonds by the corporate law firms and financial firms retained because of their so-called bankruptcy expertise. Those consultants do not consider the future issue of bonds by the issuer and do not consult with the investment bankers willing to underwrite future issues of bonds. Accordingly, they focus on resolving the rights of the issuer, current bond insurers, and bond creditors. They fail to counsel the government on available restructuring options during bankruptcy or on the best option to emerge from bankruptcy with a viable long-term bond market access structure.

The Essence of Self-Sufficiency

I consider this access to capital to be the essence of governmental self-sufficiency. To go through all the trauma and expense of bankruptcy without emerging with a ratable bond program is shameful. Settling the score between existing claimants does nothing for the taxpayers or the self-sufficiency of the bankrupt government entity. That is why a concerted consensus without bankruptcy rather than cramming down on bondholders is a superior option.

Lest anyone believe I missed the spin generated by the so-called Grand Bargain, it is true that certain philanthropies made helpful pledges and the state of Michigan also made financial commitments. But remember, the asset of the art owned by the taxpayers was bargained away at far less than market value and was not leveraged or securitized in a financing that would have created a new marketable credit for the city had it still retained ownership of the art. In fact, Kevyn Orr, former emergency manager of Detroit, in public speeches readily agreed that a speedy resolution was the priority, as the stadiums, the Joe Louis Arena, and other assets were dangled like worms on a fishline, but in my opinion, Orr and the rest of the corporate consultants never seriously considered what the bait could catch. They failed to genuinely solicit or evaluate financing options these city assets could attract.[41] Thus, bondholders and insurers had to scramble to take on other assets and accept cramdown on debts. That left the certificates of participation holders looking at the glass window of their "naked" money piled up in a pension fund.

It's a shady result at best but also an unfortunate lost opportunity. Bankruptcy counsel and financial advisors forced creditors' settlements with the bankruptcy judge's enthusiastic consent (as instructed by the governor and his schedule). They didn't pursue the option of maximum taxpayer benefit to implement a consensus restructuring of all creditors (bondholders, insurers, employees, retirees, and service vendors) and structuring a new debt program with oversight budget supervision.

This book refers to this kind of consensus approach as "old school" with principles by Alexander Hamilton and practiced by Governor Carey, among governors in Connecticut, Pennsylvania, and Rhode Island, and even Congress itself (respecting the District of Columbia). Perhaps if Anthony Williams, the first choice to come in as Detroit's "czar," had accepted that position, his experience in doing exactly that as mayor of Washington, DC, would have made the difference.[42]

In a Chapter 9 bankruptcy or a statutory federal intervention like PROMESA, the best solution to the apparent lack of taxpayer representation by counsel might be having a statutory Chapter 9 requirement to provide a trustee for the taxpayers who can also engage independent counsel. That is similar to ratepayers' advocates in many municipal utility structures. Second, I believe that Chapter 9 of that statute should be amended to require that a municipality can only become insolvent after a good faith effort has been made to restructure debt secured by all available resources or assets. (See Appendix B for the letter I wrote to the Bankruptcy Counsel after his walk-off grand slam settlement on behalf of the senior COFINA holders.)

Puerto Rico's Situation in 2019

Puerto Rico's Governor Alejandro García Padilla announced on June 28, 2015, that Puerto Rico could not pay its $72 billion in bonded debt.[43]

That led to the Puerto Rico Oversight, Management, and Economic Stability Act (PROMESA), a U.S. federal law enacted in 2016. This law established a financial oversight board, a process for restructuring debt, and expedited procedures for approving critical infrastructure projects to combat the Puerto Rican government-debt crisis.[44]

Here is the first "deal" that has been approved: The COFINA securitization of the sales tax bond was recognized by both the general obligation and senior and subordinate bondholders as well as the PROMESA board, Federal Judge Swain, and the Roselló administration as *the* preferred restructuring debt solution during this fiscal crisis. Securitization of the sales tax provides bond buyers and rating agencies with revenue-received historical data upon which to judge the value of the bonds and does not depend on balancing the general fund.

COFINA's structure had pledged to COFINA bonds that all sales tax receipts would be collected and pledged for legal coverage, with any balance not needed for debt service to flow into the island's general fund. Included in the deal with general obligation bondholders was an agreement to drop COFINA's claim to receive all sales tax revenues first and that the coverage amount would be applied to general obligation debt. In reality, the agreement was a shibboleth (empty of real meaning) or canard (rumor) to look like a compromise since the COFINA seniors actually didn't give up anything because this structure was in place under most scenarios.

In the "deal,"[45] the senior and junior COFINA bondholders and the general obligations bondholders accepted the exchange offer and received new bonds with extended maturities. However, while both experienced haircuts in the exchange, senior COFINA bondholders were cut by only 7% of the bonds' original value, while junior bond-holders were cut by 46.1%. This resulted in recovering only 53.9% of their original value. But the compromise settlement did not result in a new-money marketable bond structure.

Why? First, it is not clear that sales tax revenues would be as robust as estimated in the settlement financial plan. Tax receipts might not be enough to even pay the exchanged bonds. Second, if a bond payment default occurs, Congress could reimplement territorial control with a second version of PROMESA after PROMESA I expires in 2026.

Most important, by not resolving the legal issues judicially, any future new-money bond issue risks a repeat of the "clawback"—challenge again by the general obligation bondholders respecting those sales tax revenues.

Passing Legislation

Can Puerto Rico emerge from this fiscal fiasco confidently knowing it can reenter the bond market with a valid securitization structure? Not likely, unless fundamental changes are made. That includes creating a structure that achieves self-sufficiency by reestablishing constitutional rule of law. When the territorial status under PROMESA statute terminates, I believe there should be a fix under the U.S. Constitution —one that precludes the federal government from putting the island back into territorial status in the future. Passing a PROMESA II law would again moot the security of the revenue pledge that should protect new-money COFINA bondholders.

As part of any reemergence plan of all Commonwealth's bonds being accepted at full market value, the PROMESA board, all creditors, and U.S. Treasury officers should coordinate on passing federal legislation that would contractually commit this promise to future new-money bondholders: *The United States by an act of law may hereafter only put Puerto Rico back into territorial status when fiscal oversight is again required and only on condition of honoring the contractual obligations incurred, including new-money bonds and the settlement bonds validly issued under PROMESA.* Agreeing to that would mean all then-outstanding bondholders could invoke the Fifth Amendment—the "taking" clause of the U.S. Constitution—to protect the security of the bonds.

To summarize: Debt service schedules in the bonds taken in exchange are based on financial forecasts that are tremendously tenuous. These bonds continue to carry a risk of nonpayment. And in Puerto Rico's messy compromise, there's no assurance of a market for any new-money bonds.

Puerto Rican taxpayers need to be assured that there will be a market for its future capital needs. In my opinion, a constitutional contract would provide assurance of contract security. As to overall fiscal reform, the PROMESA board itself is under challenge. As government officials continue to contest the edicts from the board, budget reform remains unresolved.

Could Puerto Rico recover by becoming a state of the United States? Elected Puerto Rico officials tout the statehood solution as a way to protect the Commonwealth's constitution under the Tenth Amendment of the U.S. Constitution. However, due to a Puerto Rican population that overwhelmingly votes Democratic, the Republican party in Congress is unlikely to endorse statehood.

Similarities to New York Securitization

The COFINA structure of securitizing the sales tax was modeled on both the Municipal Assistance Board for New York City and its Transitional Finance Authority, both of which were challenged as violations of New York State Constitutional financial provisions and were upheld by the New York Court of Appeals. The New York and Puerto Rico constitutions are similar in asserting that general obligation bonds are entitled to receive the first state revenues upon default.

In each of the New York cases, the highest New York court recognized the authority of the legislature to exclude sales and income taxes from that pledge. That is the essence of the securitization structure. Efforts in Puerto Rico should have been devoted to having the COFINA structure validated. The goal should have been to provide long-term market acceptance for new-money COFINA bonds. It seems no one in the Puerto Rico mess has focused on this need.

In particular, the counsels to PROMESA, senior and junior COFINA, and general obligation bondholders avoided a judicial decision of the priority claim. They accepted settlement by compromise rather than a court decision that would validate the structure itself.[46]

The problem is that the litigation risk issue will still confront the first new-money COFINA bond issue. That result would be unfortunate because, unlike New York, the critical "clawback" security issue will continue to be a risk in marketing the new-money COFINA bond issue. It is clear the market will not accept that risk again or the rating agencies will even consider applying their securitization criteria to such a structure without validation.

Eager to resolve the claims of their clients, corporate bankruptcy law firms are simply not retained for the purpose of having the issuer emerge from bankruptcy with a new-money marketable bond. But isn't it essential to taxpayers to have access to the capital markets? Yes! This confirms the need for a trustee and a trustee's counsel to represent taxpayers' interests in these proceedings.

Role of Elected Officials

Supposedly, and theoretically, the taxpayers' representation in these situations are the elected officials: in Detroit, the mayor and city council, and in Puerto Rico, the governor and legislature. However, it seems clear that neither did Detroit emerge, nor is Puerto Rico emerging with viable capital market access for new capital requirements. It should be emphasized that in the fiscal crisis resolutions in New York City, Philadelphia, Scranton, Yonkers, Bridgeport,

Waterbury, District of Columbia–Congress, and in Rhode Island, the governors in charge focused on restructuring of debt with adult supervision of the municipal budget balancing to assure that the bond market would accept new financings. Bankruptcy lawyers were not battling it out for priority.

In emerging from a bankruptcy, access to capital bond markets for needed infrastructure should be the priority, but it has proven not to be—even after paying millions for consultants and settlements. Again, a taxpayer trustee coupled with its required consent to settlement might be a solution.[47] Congress should provide for such an appointment in any PROMESA statute or by a specific amendment to the Chapter 9 bankruptcy provisions.

As noted earlier, the major asset in Puerto Rico is its taxable real estate and personal property, including beautiful resorts, casinos, beaches, private apartment buildings, elaborate single-family homes, and long stretches of vacant, privately owned land available for future development. Levying a tax on these assets to restructure Puerto Rico's debts is similar to Detroit's "art collection." Unfortunately, I could not find any consultant or official who proposed tapping into it. Nor could I find any bankruptcy lawyer proposing a corporate income securitization similar to the sales tax COFINA structure as part of the bankruptcy process.

The Rights of Taxpayers

The failure of taxpayers to recognize their right and need for counsel in these fiscal workouts is glaring but not surprising, given that elected officials are supposed to represent them. However, in my opinion, violating taxpayers' interests is what Governor Alejandro García Padilla of Puerto Rico chose to do when he announced the bonded debt couldn't be paid without having explored other available restructuring options. It's unlikely he was elected with that mandate in the minds of the taxpayers.

In Detroit, the mayor was the victim of the Republican governor's decision to put Democratic Detroit into bankruptcy. In Puerto Rico, while Governor Padilla proclaimed an inability to pay without exploring options to get elected, Rosselló vacillated in his respect for the interests of employees, bondholders (particularly residents of the island), and other groups. But to me, it is a glaring fact that once elected, he never showed interest in taxing the property or income of the wealthy homeowners and major resorts, casinos, and hotel establishments.

Probably the biggest failure is the federal judiciary as a fact of fairness not recognizing and requiring a taxpayer trustee and counsel, knowing that neither the mayor of Detroit or governor of Michigan nor the governor of Puerto Rico could be counted on to represent or protect resident taxpayers when the assets of the wealthy are at risk. Just like the concept of preserving the art collection for its cultural value to the region was ruled out of bounds to the Detroit creditors, the personal and real property and income of the wealthy have been rendered "unavailable" as resources to pay Puerto Rico debt.

Illicit Success Fees

In Puerto Rico, the litigation and settlement talks are still ongoing. Do you know that the law firms, financial advisory firms, and lobbyists have built into their retainers a so-called success fee? For example, this amounts to millions of dollars calculated on a percentage of the COFINA holders' haircut. Higher fees have gone to senior COFINA lawyers, financial consultants, and lobbyists (at 93 percent) compared to that of the junior COFINA professionals (at 46 percent).

The senior COFINA lawyers are entitled to monthly fees of $55,000 and potentially a success fee of up to $3,000,000.[48] This fee is not based on time spent; rather, it's an incentive to settle at the best price for the hedge fund client. However, this type of fee has never been part of municipal bond issues and, in my view, should be ruled as being against public policy in a governmental bankruptcy. I consider it an illicit use of money for a private purpose.

I have been representing both underwriters of state and local bond issues and as bond counsel representing the issuers for more than fifty years. In that time, I never came across the concept of charging "success fees." The concept crossed over from corporate bankruptcies and has not been challenged as "an abuse against public finance policy" by either the elected officials of Puerto Rico or the federal appointees of the PROMESA Oversight Board or the federal judiciary. In my view, it should be.

Why is that? The cost for consultants would be in the multi-millions, making it the most expensive municipal bankruptcy ever (even if adjusted for inflation). It will probably never be exceeded in any future municipal bankruptcy. In addition, unless their validity is challenged by the United States Treasury, PROMESA Board, the courts, or the territory of Puerto Rico in the Puerto Rico proceedings, "success fees" will undoubtedly become a standard charge in governmental bankruptcies.

A Waste of Money

The controversy concerning whether or not the COFINA pledge of taxes is subject to the "clawback provision of the Puerto Rico constitution" was compromised. Accordingly, there is no legal precedent to rely on in future COFINA or general obligation bond issue. Hence, the risk must be disclosed in such offerings. As a result, a penalty interest will be included in every future bond sale, assuming the bonds are marketable *at all* with such a well-known major risk. The major defect of this process can only be explained by the absence of counseling to all parties about the basics of public finance. At the very least, the desired outcome of any municipal bankruptcy should be the *development of a marketable, secure new-money bond structure.*

Here, the statutory pledge was neither validated nor invalidated; neither was any marketable security feature added to the general obligation structure. We do not know if enough island-wide statutory personal and real property tax is available to support the general obligation bond faith and credit pledge.

To summarize, the silence of the municipal finance industry on this issue is deafening, and the apparent ignorance of the consultants for the general obligation bondholders is embarrassing. What's the only logical explanation? That the politically powerful voices prevailed.

Finally, once again, average resident taxpayers were improperly represented during the entire Detroit and Puerto Rico proceedings. In each case, the governor chose to retain corporate bankruptcy counsel and announced, without prior approval or a mandate from the tax-payers, that the outstanding bonded debt could not be paid. Neither governor, I suggest, considered the fact that the "willingness to pay debt" was an asset that was being wasted by that pronouncement. I would doubt that the retained bankruptcy law firms even raised that point.

The "old school" governors included Governor Carey in New York, several governors in Connecticut, Pennsylvania, and New Jersey, and state treasurer (then and now governor of Rhode Island) and Congress itself with respect to the District of Columbia. They understood market access was critical and chose a cooperative, consensus restructuring as the alternative to bankruptcy. Thus, where elected leaders default on their duty to the taxpayers, fairness requires these taxpayers have a voice—and a right to counsel. That's because no one—including the federally appointed PROMESA board, the elected governor and elected legislators, or any of the well-paid professional consultants—saw fit to restore the island's creditworthiness. They should have restructured its debt by validating a market-acceptable bond program. Perhaps everyone thinks that funds made available from the federal government for hurricane relief will be sufficient for the island's capital needs. They're not.

The proof of the failure to focus on restoring access to the capital bond market can best be summarized by knowing that almost all of the nine-billion-dollar infrastructure projects are stalled. That is despite the fact that the federal statute PROMESA actually included and provided a methodology for continuing them.[49] In other words, while the federal judge was signing off on the settlement exchange compromise between existing general obligation and COFINA holders, the taxpayers' need for financing these projects was not even being considered. Taxpayer representation would have prevented any settlements between creditors unless access to capital markets for new essential projects was assured.

Recent panels convened at a conference focused on the debauchery of the principle of "willingness to pay" in Puerto Rico and reiterated the new risks associated by municipal bonds. That included an upsetting legal decision by the federal judiciary in one of the Puerto Rico cases that questioned the priority of special revenue pledges, which adversely affected revenue bonds everywhere. It also includes the collusion of the federal government with the governor in passing the PROMESA legislation. This permitted Puerto Rico to repudiate its debt as contracted in the bond documents.

Can a State Go Bankrupt?

Could the governor of a state collude with the federal government to pass bankruptcy legislation permitting voluntary filing by a state? Obviously, the concern is that a state may "will" a similar result as Puerto Rico to file for bankruptcy and this or any president and Congress will "find a way" to permit that to happen by amending Chapter 9 of the Federal Bankruptcy Act. The municipal bond industry should then (and even now with a substantial campaign) lobby for precluding the stripping of bondholders' and taxpayers' rights by expanding the insolvency test. It would include cash available from market resources such as restructuring of debt (a test that might have precluded each of three bankruptcies—Orange County, Detroit, and Puerto Rico) and a requirement that the bankruptcy court (upon filing but before proceeding cause counsel and financial advisor to be retained on behalf of the taxpayers) to manage the solicitation of a bond market offering of restructured bonds. This would be done in exchange for outstanding bonds or otherwise it would be an essential consent to any settlement.

Citizens Served Badly

The first critique coming out of the COFINA settlement confirms my position that the taxpaying citizens on that island have been badly served by the PROMESA process. The federal court and the PROMESA board approved the settlement between general obligation and COFINA bondholders in which hedge funds did very well. But clearly, the resources from the sales tax have been allocated to debt service for the newly issued COFINA bonds exchanged for senior and subordinate COFINA and debt service for the outstanding general obligation (GO) bonds.

In other words, there are no revenues from the sales tax reserved for anticipated debt service for new bonds needed for current capital structures. The taxpayers simply were not consulted or considered. The millions paid to lawyers, lobbyists, and financial consultants benefited only their clients. Since the taxpayers were not represented, nothing of the pie was cut for them. That is not how a governmental bankruptcy is intended to work. (See summary of taxpayer loss here.[50])

The ghosts of Hamilton and Governor Carey should soldier on.[51]

Note: Recent commentary by an economist concludes, in effect, that Puerto Rico will not emerge from bankruptcy with any access to capital markets to fulfill new infrastructure requirements in spite of the millions of dollars spent on litigation, lobbyists, and consultants.[52] The settlement between the COFINA and GO bondholders, which resulted in newly issued sales tax bonds and an allocation of the sales tax to secure GO bonds, took all the revenues estimated (in an aggressive, speculative analysis) and left no room for new debt service for new bonds.[53] Both the PROMESA oversight board and federal judge, Judge Swain, seem captivated by the bankruptcy lawyers by focusing only on settling existing creditor disputes. They both failed to appreciate that, first and foremost, the taxpayers and residents of Puerto Rico need a return to self-sufficiency, meaning balanced budgets and access to capital markets for new required capital infrastructure.

In other words, the bankruptcy can be judged as a totally wasted opportunity and expensive fiscal disaster, leaving the island with no obvious resources as leverage to entice new bond investors. The federal government will need to continue with hurricane grants and other politically labeled programs to camouflage the federal bailout assistance that will be required. Despite the Obama administration promising that PROMESA would not be a federal bailout, under the Trump administration, there has been no Treasury leadership to counter this adverse result.[54] In the view of this author, the island will remain a federal controlled territory for a generation or more.

Undoubtedly, this chapter on Puerto Rico is not the last word. Ongoing matters necessarily require watching for newsworthy updates. For example, a July 2019 article in *The New York Times* noted that "Puerto Rico's financial collapse led Congress to create a way for the territory to restructure its debt. If it succeeds, states struggling with pension costs might seek a similar option."[55] That's why monitoring this issue is critical.

Obviously, with respect to Puerto Rico, with what appears to be a taxpayer revolt arising from the revulsion of reading Roselló's emails, a new administration might consider the realistic option of creating a new marketable bond secured by a tax on personal and real property as the solution to self-sufficiency for that island.

PART TWO

Everyday Life and Public Finance

CHAPTER 6

Financing Toll Roads

This chapter highlights the difficulties of developing a twenty-first century solution to the financing requirements for the transportation needs of the states and nation.

New Jersey Governor Jon Corzine had been the state's U.S. senator and before that a chairman of Goldman Sachs. In 2008, New Jersey issued a Request for Proposals (RFP) for counsel to develop plans for any public private partnerships that would benefit the state. My colleagues and I at Hawkins put together a team to respond to this RFP.

My young partner Eric Petersen and I believed that public-private partnerships (P3s)[56] was a term newly coined by corporate firms seeking retainers by states due to their expertise in corporate finance. The leaders of these firms sanctimoniously believed public finance lawyers were unprepared for joint venture partnerships.

It is true that public finance lawyers aren't entirely familiar with corporate tax laws, corporate structures, or corporate profit motivated documentation. But it's also true that—based on our experience with most of the major corporate lawyers in structuring the MAC bond issue for the 1975 NYC fiscal crisis—those corporate firms know little about state and municipal law. Even worse, they don't know that they don't know. For example, they assumed uncomplicated public finance structures.

What many of these firms chose not to know is that Eric and I and certain other public finance firms had practically invented the public-private partnership structure. We had done this to provide a public finance solution to a basic service of government—namely, garbage or solid waste disposal. We had become experts in drafting twenty- to thirty-year contractual arrangements with companies that claimed proprietary expertise in burning solid waste to produce energy for sale to utilities. We had become highly experienced not only in drafting statutes in states authorizing those contractual arrangements on a sole source or competitive bid option but also in negotiating those contracts with top law firms. These firms included Debevoise Plimpton, Sullivan & Cromwell, and Phillips Nizer, as well as other big-named law firms representing the companies or public utilities.

Governor Corzine, who came from the corporate side of Goldman, seemed to favor hiring a corporate firm, Skadden Arps.[57] Through the interview process, it had become clear to Nancy Feldman Director of Public Finance in the New Jersey Treasurer's office that the Hawkins team had not only current credentials in P3s but we also knew our way around New Jersey public finance law. Hawkins' public finance partners had written most of the municipal finance laws in the 1930s. In fact, they created and counseled many of the established authorities such as the New Jersey Turnpike Authority.

Also, Eric and I presented sample documentation already drafted regarding the contractual provisions and risk issues such as change in law, force majeure, cost overruns, labor disputes, change orders, etc., that would be the essence of any negotiations. So there we were, hired as co-counsel with Skadden advising the state of New Jersey on P3s. Our first assignment was to develop a list of all state functions that could be eligible for private sector management. Some called this political initiative "outsourcing"; others called it union busting; others thought of it as better budgeting. In reality, it was clear that, through the present valuing of the future income stream of the selected enterprise, Corzine would have access to present dollars. He would use those dollars to dramatically rebuild infrastructure, provide ready dollars for new capital structures, and balance the budget without adding new tax increases. At the same time, the state would produce revenues in excess of what it was then receiving from tax revenues. "Monetization of public assets" became the buzz word.

New Jersey Lottery

First on our list to explore a P3 was the New Jersey Lottery. The state wasn't aggressively marketing the lottery; the number of ticket outlets was inadequate; and not much advertising of the payoff potential was in place. A lottery run by businesspeople motivated by a profit would be better managed.

Playing the lottery is like imposing a regressive tax on the poorer segment of society induced by the fantasy of a big payoff. It is sponsored by the state mostly to provide a legal option to the so-called "numbers" managed by the mafia in many states. The addictive attraction to the chance of winning has been documented from early Roman and Greek times. In the United States and in almost every other civilized nation, having a lottery is illegal except for a national lottery. In the U.S., no national lottery exists, although at least one has skirted the rules such that it operates like a national lottery. Each state (by federal law) is authorized to operate only one state lottery.

We quickly found and reviewed a U.S. Department of Justice opinion that a state lottery could not be "privatized" and therefore could not be managed by a private firm. The games themselves are designed by private firms but not the lotteries' managements or operations. Both Skadden and Hawkins[58] concurred, but Skadden spent time to run the opinion of the Justice Department "up and down the flagpole" to make sure no variation of a P3 could be construed as eligible. Hawkins realized that no securitization of lottery revenues could happen without a challenge from the Justice Department. Therefore, any financing would be delayed beyond the governor's timeline for achieving the present-valued funding.

Toll Roads

Both firms selected the next item for securitization review to be the toll roads: New Jersey Turnpike, Garden State Parkway, and the Atlantic City Expressway. Excellent economic and political reasons could be stated for why these roads were ideal for monetization through a P3.

First, the well-publicized first-in-the-nation public-private turnpike partnership had been quarterbacked by the Republican governor of Indiana, Mitch Daniels. Over a sixty-year period, the present value of tolling for the Indiana Turnpike generated $3 billion for the state—enough to cover the cost of constructing the state road capital improvements for the next ten years or so.

Second, at some point, a governor of New Jersey had persuaded the state legislature to provide explicit executive oversight control of the New Jersey Turnpike Authority by legislating a gubernatorial veto over the board minutes of the Authority. As a result of this veto power, the governor became politically saddled with any increase in tolls. As a result, the actual tolls had not been increased in years. In fact, the amounts were enough to cover debt service on outstanding bonds but well below what was needed to support even an average level of needed maintenance.

New Jersey Governor Corzine wanted us to develop a more politically palatable proposal than the Indiana toll road while delivering a large present value to provide a capital transportation fund. In the Indiana P3, Indiana had sold its turnpike management and ownership under a sixty-year concession agreement to an Australian bank. This generated adverse publicity about having an "alien" bank involved in the state's major road. Having foreign banks such as the Royal Bank of Scotland, Royal Bank of Canada, or Barclays Bank from England come into the U.S. seemed politically acceptable. But it was deemed too much to have an actual infrastructure operation such as this major turnpike under a foreign-owned profit-motivated concession.

Despite tax breaks such as depreciation that comes with private corporate assets, this kind of ownership required a corporate rate of return on its investment amount and would operate for a "profit"— another concept alien to public infrastructure.

Indiana Governor Mitch Daniels had managed politically to authorize the transaction in a fast-tracked legislative process, but the intense public criticism that followed made it unwise to replicate the Indiana model elsewhere. New Jersey had become accustomed to public authorities[59] (e.g., New Jersey Turnpike Authority, Meadowlands Sports Authority, New Jersey State Housing Finance Authority), but they were publicly owned and operated on a nonprofit basis by appointees of the executive branch. These authorities didn't need to answer to shareholders who would demand dividends at a corporate rate of return for their investments.

Hawkins brought to the working group a legal solution by proposing and developing a public finance tax-exempt structure. It proposed forming a not-for-profit corporation that would be managed like a public hospital or university by public-spirited citizens. The corporation would be separate from the state and not be legally subject to the control of the state. To its credit, Skadden found a similar nonprofit structure modeled after a Canadian precedent, but it hadn't been vetted for financing on a tax-exempt basis under U.S. federal tax rules.

In tandem, the two firms developed the documentation for organizing the nonprofit and the financing structure for issuing tax-exempt bonds. They also developed the process for the solicitation of a private management company with the expertise for managing the three roads. This was done under a so-called qualified management contract subject to the federal tax-exempt bonding regulations. The proposed nonprofit, like an authority, would not have shareholders as a private corporation does. Thus, it would not need to achieve a rate of return or the interest rate as demanded by investors in taxable structures. And it would have directors from New Jersey, not from a foreign country. And most important, the nonprofit would not be "related" to the state (in technical Internal Revenue Service jargon), so the higher-interest outstanding bonds of the existing authorities could be current or advance refunded at lower tax-exempt rates. This refunding would produce a larger present value, allowing the governor to boost his infrastructure fund.

The consultants had counted on Governor Corzine's political and financial skills to "sell" this proposal and concept to state voters and elected legislators. However, his failure to do so can be directly attributed to sixty years of the toll regime being embedded in the proposed not-for-profit concession. In other words, to "sell" the roads to gain present value dollars for road improvements over the next ten years, the nonprofit would have to provide investors with sixty years of revenues from tolls. The tolls were initially set to show coverage for level debt service and current operating expenses. These would increase annually by a cost-of-living index. Such an automatic annual toll increase was built into the concession agreement, obviating any annual political influence. However, the editorial boards and public hearing objections spelled complete rejection of the proposed nonprofit securitization of the New Jersey toll roads.

The sequel to this privatization story is most interesting. The sale price of the Indiana Turnpike to the private Australian bank turned out to be too high for that bank. Even with the escalation of toll fees, the turnpike was losing money, so the bank's subsidiary filed for bankruptcy under federal bankruptcy laws. To mitigate the damages for the bondholders of the subsidiary, the bankruptcy court conducted an auction of the remaining fifty-five years on the concession agreement.

At that time, I had moved on from Hawkins to develop a national finance practice for state and local bond issues at another firm. There, I thought the nonprofit structure would work well for the Indiana Turnpike and perhaps be the successful bid. My new partners and I put together a group led by local towns along the route of the turnpike, qualifying as a bidder. The bankruptcy court had hired the same firm that worked on the New Jersey project as finance advisors. The bankruptcy committee was made aware of the extensive research supporting our proposal. As a result, the committee expedited qualifying our group as a bidder. We were confident it would be better than that of any group having a taxable structure.

Unfortunately, we lost; but why?

First, two bids were over $5 billion, which meant the bankrupt entity would recover its initial investment and then some. Second, the group that bid a taxable structure placed it at the lowest price and was a poor third place. Our not-for-profit group was just $200 million lower than the winning bid. The highest-price bid (and therefore the winning bid) was submitted by a consortium of pension funds, including the prestigious CALPERS of California.

This marked development of a brand-new resource of funds for governmental infrastructure. The long-term ownership of a "safe" infrastructure and a seasoned concession with toll increases proved to be a valuable asset for a pension fund portfolio. The pension fund did not need either taxable or tax-exempt financing for its bid. That's because it had readily available pension funds to use for the purchase and, unlike the risk profile of shopping centers or office buildings, an ongoing main street road like the Indiana Turnpike would always be needed. Thus, its market was assured, and the toll regime for the remaining fifty-five years was continuing in place.

Public-Private Partnerships in Place

Currently, many public-private partnerships have been placed in service since 2001. They've been created for all types of revenue-producing public infrastructure including for solid waste-to-energy and sewage treatment plants, water supply systems, and even desalination of water from the Pacific Ocean by the San Diego Water Authority. Many of those concession agreements are with companies from foreign countries (particularly several from France). The primary motivation (except those with a technology innovation) appears to be replacing an expensive union operating contract. Others, though, have considered the expertise of being managed privately preferable to public management.

It is shocking that the Trump administration has not focused on or introduced any legislation to rebuild American infrastructure by tapping into similar proven financing structures that would attract investments from pension funds and the municipal bond market.

CHAPTER 7

Water Treatment and Public Finance

This chapter highlights examples of how public finance contributed to the viability of water treatment plants. It features examples from Michigan, Connecticut, and New York.

The delivery of clean drinking water to the populace is one of the wonders of the engineering world (think about the aqueducts constructed in ancient times by the Romans). In Michigan, the Lake Huron intake facility was deliberately made oversized to not only service the Detroit region but to potentially transmit water to the Southwest. Two tunnels built in the nineteenth century served New York City despite its enormous growth through all of the twentieth century.

In certain states such as Connecticut and New Jersey, ownership of private water systems—sometimes by deed from the king of England— was part of the practical development of commerce. In New Jersey, former Governor Tom Kean was descended from one of those owner- ship families. He derived his wealth from owning a private New Jersey water company.

In Connecticut, the private stock–owned New Haven Water Company was formed in the 1850s to provide water to the Greater New Haven region. Its source was several water reservoirs protected by plenty of surrounding pristine forestry acres and zoned and fenced off completely from any housing or commercial developments and also from camping or fishing options. Accordingly, the system fully relied on the "technology" of natural flow purification.

Natural Purification No Longer Viable

In the 1980s, the federal Environmental Protection Agency (EPA) determined that natural purification could no longer be counted on as sufficient treatment nationwide. Developers were encroaching everywhere, and run-offs from shopping center parking lots were spilling into the streams that historically had carried only melted snow. Expensive treatment facilities were being mandated.

New Haven, Connecticut, home to Yale University, has a sophisticated citizenry that understood how a tremendous amount of forestry land had served as their city water's purification process. But with the EPA regulations, this land would be rendered obsolete for that purpose. Inevitably, a private water company would find a profitable use for the land such as developing it for residential or commercial use.

So New Haven's citizens took action. They formed the South Central Regional Water Authority to buy out the private water company. This would stop commercial development of the forestry lands around the ten reservoirs serving the greater New Haven region.[60] The Authority retained Goldman Sachs (GS) to manage the bond offering, and I was retained to serve as counsel to the underwriting team formed by GS.

GS advised that purchasing the stock rather than purchasing the assets of the New Haven Water Company would achieve the best pricing for the Authority. (How the accounting is treated between a purchase of the assets versus a stock purchase is always decided as precondition basis when buying out for-profit stockholding companies. A public authority would normally opt for the purchase of stock because it does not have the tax benefits of depreciating of assets that a private owner would have.[61])

The initial stock bid of approximately $65 a share was based on an analysis of a going water supply concern,[62] *and* it was consistent with past valuations and operations of the New Haven Water Company. However, that offer was rejected almost immediately. It became obvious that the Authority's board was motivated to preserve open space around the reservoir, but this motivation was matched by the Water Company board's desire to maximize the value of those development rights. Final pricing ended up at $92 a share, which resulted in a significant increase in water rates. The increase was considered worthwhile, though, because the Authority would preserve the beautiful forestry land as open space. And the increase in water rates was mitigated to some degree because the Authority, unlike the private water company, did not charge beyond expenses. In other words, it did not seek a profit or have a rate of return on equity requirement, and its interest rate on the bonds to buy the stock would be tax exempt.

As the underwriter's counsel, I was responsible for drafting the bond offering document.[63] A "dam" engineer—a term that always evoked a smile—was responsible for disclosing information about the state of the dams and quality of the water. Unfortunately, certain EPA-required nomenclature presented a disclosure dilemma. For instance, the phrase "hazardous" dam would inaccurately convey to bond investors the sense that a dam was in terrible physical shape. But this phrase doesn't describe the characteristics of the infrastructure; it refers to its location near population centers. The dams located within range of flooding densely populated areas such as New Haven received that label.

As an aside, suggested business uses for the land surrounding the dams included the Authority going into the cemetery business. After researching that issue, we quickly discouraged that option after learning that one of the most egregious examples of polluting water came from leakage of embalming fluid from coffins.

What About the Tenth Dam?

Doing a final review before the offering document was mailed, I noticed only nine of the ten dams were listed for acquisition. I called the "dam" engineer, and he apologized. He had been assigned to call me and explain that one of the dams was not in good shape. Because of that, the Authority had decided not to buy it. I asked if it was serious enough to cause a flood requiring boots, row boats, or what. He responded, "Coast Guard."

Yes, I learned it *was* one of those "hazardous" dams that could flood a dense residential area of New Haven. Then I asked how much it would cost to fix it. After he replied, "Ten million dollars," I told him to include $12 million more in the bond issue.

There was no way the underwriters could allow this Authority to acquire all assets *except one* of this private company and not be exposed to the liability incurred if that one asset caused extensive damage. This was especially true because there was no provision in the sale document for escrowing or holding back any percentage of the sale price. The stockholders would presumably dissolve the corporation and distribute the proceeds of sale to its individual holders.

Using this "common sense corporate law counseling," we were able to avert that problem.

Water Treatment in New York State

A conflict between development pressure and water treatment plants played out quite differently in New York than in Connecticut.

In 1995, the first year of Governor George Pataki's administration, the EPA ordered New York City to build ten treatment facilities along certain upstate flow points to cleanse the water flowing from upstate New York to NYC.[64] In an extraordinarily technical but sophisticated and expedited negotiation, the governor's counsel, Michael C. Finnegan, secured a multiparty agreement to protect the watershed from waste runoff. In 1995, the New York City Watershed Agreement he brokered was approved by the EPA, municipalities, upstate developers, New York City, and the state.[65]

In essence, the state would acquire prescribed development rights along the watershed and thereby preclude the need for treatment facilities. It was understood that, unlike Connecticut where seepage into the dams due to development beyond the forestry land could not be curbed without treatment plants, the length of the water flow from upstate New York could continue as a purification process. This would be true as long as development along the route was restricted.

CHAPTER 8

Successful UConn 2000 Project

Perhaps my most creative contribution to public finance was the development of the financing structure that solved the capital facilities rehabilitation and expansion needs of Connecticut's flagship college, the University of Connecticut. It's described in this chapter.

The University of Connecticut (UConn) started as an agricultural college in the northeast corner of the state—a rural area that, for years, had received funding for each new infrastructure by lobbying the state legislature. The university did so annually, asking to be included in the state general obligation bond program featuring particular projects such as a new library, new lab, or new dormitory. UConn competed with all other state agencies for the bonding authority as well as the Department of Public Works' priority construction schedule.

At one point in the 1990s, it became clear to Connecticut Speaker of the House Tom Ritter, a UConn graduate, that a better system was needed. The focus centered on Babbidge Library, the symbol of the university's crumbling infrastructure. It was expected to have large cost overruns with delays from construction and building flaws showing up. Speaker Ritter arranged for me to be retained by the state treasurer to draft proposed legislation and meet regularly with certain members of the Board of Trustees who had financing acumen. We went to work that summer in 1994 in our Hartford conference room. Our task was to be completed before Governor John Rowland's administration took office in January 1995.

The group agreed that the capital needs of the university at its Storrs campus included major rehabilitation of buildings and expansion of new teaching and residential facilities costing more than a billion dollars. To group members, it became clear the pattern of authorizing about one hundred million dollars a year and then prioritizing and naming each project for that year was outdated. So mirroring a communist country's terminology, I proposed the UConn 2000 program.[66] It was a ten-year billion-dollar program that named all projects to be covered during the upcoming decade while leaving the priority, planning, and building detail to the university's board but limiting the amount that could be bonded to $100 million each fiscal year.

Clearly, the benefits of UConn 2000 changed everything related to infrastructure for the university. Staff members could do their "real" work rather than lobbying and prioritizing each year. As well, the design and preliminary engineering, road rerouting, sewer and water mains, etc., could be done at the beginning for all the named projects. This represented a substantial cost savings. Knowing the physical campus was well funded, students could anticipate living in rehabilitated or new residential facilities, and faculty members could accept job offers and assist in designing their labs in a rehabilitated or new building.

Most important, the statute authorized UConn to establish its own public works unit, thus relieving the Connecticut Department of Public Works of responsibility for all construction on any of the UConn campuses.[67] Subsequently, the legislature adopted UConn 21st Century, authorizing a second billion-dollar ten-year program and then a third one-and-a-half billion multiyear building program.

In 2009, this flagship university broke into being one of the twenty best in the country. The nation's champion women's basketball team, led in 1995 by All-American Rebecca Lobo, also persuaded first-year Governor Rowland to support passage of UConn 2000. The belief behind it was that if UConn could establish itself as the number-one national basketball team, it could make similar strides in education.

Executing the ten-year capital planning concept transformed the entire physical campus and provided the proper support to attract both students and faculty. Plus it was based on a logical shift. Before 1995, the state had bonded about a hundred million dollars a year with project-by-project authorization. Committing to a capital ten-year program was the key to the success of UConn 2000.

Excerpted is the report written at the end of the first ten years.[68]

For years, surveys of students who were accepted, but who chose not to attend UConn said the physical condition of the campus was a primary reason for going elsewhere. (Many of these students were Connecticut residents who then left the state; Connecticut is the second highest state exporter of college students nationally after Alaska.) The quality of academic buildings and on-campus housing was consistently cited as a significant reason for choosing not to enroll, and the surveys showed that prospective students lacked confidence in the academic program as a result of the poor impression left by the University's physical state. UCONN 2000 is helping to slow the "brain drain."

Rebuilding, Restoring and Enhancing UConn's Facilities: Even before the close of the program's first phase, a profound physical transformation has already taken place at the University's main and regional campuses. Since 1995, 97 construction and renovation projects have been completed; 51 are currently underway. At Storrs, the major projects that are completed include the Chemistry building, South Campus dormitories, North Campus Parking Garage, the integration of modern technology into curriculum. Construction is underway on the Biological Sciences building, the Agricultural

Biotechnology building, and the Fine Arts building; groundbreaking for the School of Business Administration building will take place this spring.

The main campus at Storrs has been rethought in accordance with a new Master Plan. In 1998, a pedestrian core was put in place, featuring a new central mall with plazas and major crosswalks that signal the heart of campus. Less visible but critical improvements to the University's backbone infrastructure—roadway, transportation, utility and information technology networks—are completed or underway. Similar transformations are completed or taking place at the University's regional campuses. A new campus in downtown Stamford opened in January 1998. Design is done on the agricultural facility at the Torrington campus and upgrades at the Great Hartford and Waterbury campuses are planned. An already enhanced School of Law campus has further improvements in the planning stage. Utility infrastructure improvements, a new marine science building, and extensive renovations to Branford House are underway at Avery Point.

What did we learn from that solution? That a university can have greater control over its future through creative financing practices. To its detriment, a state can get trapped in standard financing practices that preclude priorities and proper allocation of its financial resources. Hence, the UConn 2000 program provided the university with control over its capital program. However, given that tuition and other fees and charges cannot fully sustain its operation and debt service on UConn bonds, it did not relieve the state of providing the credit of the state to support the bond financing,

The key was to recognize that the state had been bonding for UConn at about a hundred million dollars a year, but this approach was based on the passage of each project and its cost. By bundling all projects into ten-year increments, UConn became an efficient education engine, with its campuses modernized and up to date technically.

CHAPTER 9

Waste-to-Energy Projects: First Public/Private Partnerships

This chapter reflects the first financings of what are now called private-public partnerships. It discusses the risks that private companies are willing to take to become involved in the infrastructure projects subject to smart, profit-motivated management based on a reasonable rate structure and patented technology.

This chapter also chronicles the multiyear effort by New York City to solve its dumping problems. They were finally resolved by NYC committing to transport waste to host landfill communities in the neighboring states of Pennsylvania and Ohio. (Tertiary lining of landfills has become environmentally acceptable and readily permitted under the rules of the Environmental Protection Agency and various state environmental regulatory bodies. As noted in this chapter section, the history of the technology of incinerators precluded building a waste-to-energy facility in NYC.)

I n the 1980s, every population center was confronting the enormous harm to the environment caused by dumping unsorted garbage (solid waste) into the landfills. These were becoming major hills, mostly hidden from the public view. There were those who were visually obvious as mountains of waste being built such as along the New Jersey Turnpike, Fresh Kills in Staten Islands, and along interstate highways outside New Haven and Hartford, for example.

What happened to change this? A twenty-year public finance industry effort to successfully develop a financing private-public partnership framework to site, build, and operate waste-to-energy plants. The municipalities involved contractually committed to deliver waste to plants that incinerated and converted (pursuant to privately patented and owned technology) solid waste to energy for sale to investor owned utilities. This effort involved Long Island and several upstate New York counties as well as municipalities in Connecticut, Florida, California, Pennsylvania, and Illinois.

The solid waste disposal initiative marked the start of the search for alternative energy that has produced wind, sun, and water turbines over recent years.

Increased Need for Landfills

The early 1980s marked a period of increased public awareness of the growing need for landfills.[69] Excessive packaging of consumer goods and proliferation of plastic encasings in a throwaway society resulted in opening landfills or even creating higher hills of solid waste on existing landfills. The unsightliness of landfills caused many to be surrounded by high fencing and located well away from frequently used roads. In addition, it became clear that leaching from solid waste decomposition was harming the groundwater. This occurred to such an extent that both federal and local environmental agencies converged on regulations to close landfills over a prescribed schedule.

At the same time, they encouraged recycling and other methods of reducing the amount of solid waste generated.

The state of Connecticut adopted a comprehensive policy well ahead of other states and, with state credit enhancement, it financed infrastructure facilities known as waste-to-energy facilities.[70] The idea was to truck the solid waste picked up by municipal and private haulers to waste-to-energy facilities (either privately owned or licensed to operate). These plants burned the waste, producing energy to sell to investor owned or public utilities at a price fixed and mandated by state statute.

First, state administrators hired First Boston Corporation to produce a feasibility report on the market reception of buying bonds to finance this new technology. As a result of the report, the state created the Connecticut Resource Recovery Authority (CRRA) with the goal of financing five or more such facilities and producing about 25 percent of the energy needed in the state of Connecticut. I had been retained by the state's treasurer to draft the statutory authorization for bonds to be issued with state credit enhancement based on a finding of "self-sufficiency" by the board. This Authority successfully procured, financed, and built four of these plants that are in good working operation today.

Formidable Negotiation

However, it was a formidable legal negotiation. Developing a new technology meant having to balance the interests of the public and private sectors as well as the rewards and risks of joint venturing while assuring the risks are properly allocated. Twenty years later, the municipal bond industry began using the term private-public partnership primarily for the private management of toll roads. But in reality, those of us who developed the legal structure for these waste-to-energy plants had already pioneered a financial format.

The project financings were deemed unique because of a confluence of factors. Burning solid waste to produce energy was a new technology that the governmental sector had to procure from one of a few private companies. Each company had various patent protections in place, and municipalities had the responsibility to ensure that the solid waste disposal each claimed was through the "best" technology. With "encouragement" from the public service commission and/or state-mandated pricing, investor-owned utilities had to purchase the produced power under long-term contracts. The landfills, relieved of the volume of solid waste being burned, were expected to accept the "residue" from the incinerated waste. As an economic symmetry, it all made sense. But the negotiations among the parties to allocate the risk and rewards proved difficult.

First Procurement

The first procurement for a facility in Bridgeport was instructive for all future deals. The technology selected had been patented by a start-up company that reduced the waste to pellets, much like coal. However, the company didn't have creditworthy resources, so my client, CRRA, insisted it partner with another company that had a sufficient credit standing. Presumably, this arrangement could provide financial backing for any cost overruns and would meet the statutory requirement of "self-sufficiency."

Recognizing a new source of fuel and an opportunity to be a first in the nation on that product, Occidental Petroleum agreed to be the partner. The underwriter, First Boston, selected Sullivan & Cromwell as its counsel. We at Hawkins were retained as finance counsel on the major negotiations for the concession agreement on behalf of a newly created Authority. We had drafted the state statute creating the state authority and authorizing such transactions. In addition, as the condition precedent to the issuance of the bonds, we inserted that the board certify that expected net revenues were enough to pay the debt service on the bonds and the operating cost of the facility net of revenues from the sale of power, so the state's guarantee would not likely be invoked.

To demonstrate that the guarantee wouldn't be invoked, we explained the need for a "self-sufficiency test." Note that our client, the Authority, was a conduit with no assets. It could not take the risk that the technology would fail to pass a three-month commercial operation testing period. First Boston asserted that bondholders wouldn't take that risk, either.

We had negotiated with and had the wealthy communities of Fairfield County (including Darien, Westport, and Greenwich) "put" their waste to the plant and pay. This was conditional upon the service, and it was subject to reasonable pricing. In other words, the municipalities would not take the risk of a "force majeure" (acts of God such as hurricanes or unforeseen circumstances such as labor or supply disputes) shutting down the plant for a time.

Another source of money and risk-taking was the emerging venture capital investors. The rate of return for taking that risk would need to be more than 20 percent, resulting in a tipping fee too high for the communities to accept. Hence, it fell to the deep pockets of the partner Occidental to accept the technology risk. This included meeting the tough commercial operation test (COT) and incurring additional financing for either a force majeure delay in meeting the commercial operations date (COD) or to make any needed improvements to pass the COT.

The CRRA offered to issue $50 million in bonds to finance this facility. Because (1) the construction contract covered the guarantee of Occidental Petroleum (respecting both the COT and COD); (2) operations were secured by the "Put and Pay" contract of the Fairfield County municipalities; and (3) the IOU, United Illuminating, was mandated at a statutory price to purchase the energy, First Boston found a ready market of bond buyers.

Paying Off the Bonds

However, within two years, flaws in the technology became apparent. Representing CRRA was Jay Jackson from the attorney general's office; Charley Stroh, a country lawyer from the town of Suffield named CRRA chairman by Governor Meskill; and me. We found ourselves in the pristine New York offices of perhaps the most renowned lawyer of that era, Louis Nizer, counsel to Occidental.

The waste facility had repeatedly failed to pass the COT, thereby requiring the company to pay off the bonds under the explicit language of the contract. The controversy never got to litigation because Mr. Stroh had the patience and persistence to listen to Mr. Nizer's stories of his successes while drinking wine in his office.

Meanwhile, Mr. Nizer's associates and other partners kept trying to find an "out" in the fine print of the contract. Mr. Nizer finally capitulated at lunch at his table at the Algonquin Hotel restaurant and gave Mr. Stroh a sketch of his profile drawn on the paper tablecloth. He also handed over a check from Occidental in the amount of fifty million dollars.

Lessons Learned

The lessons learned from both the private and the governmental sector vantage (or disadvantage) viewpoints were substantial. In particular, First Boston had retained Ricardo Mestres of Sullivan & Cromwell as its counsel. He had drafted an ironclad COT that worked in practice, because while the pellets did burn, the furnace did not work under the sustained thirty-day burn activity. Nobody was able to devise a technical fix.

In this process, we learned that the "self-sustaining standard" must be without exception; otherwise, commercial defenses of corporations, such as impossibility of performances, could be properly asserted to avoid liability.

The selfsufficiency declaration proved to be an excellent point in the negotiation with Combustion Engineering (CE), the company selected to build the waste-to-energy plant that would service the disposal of solid waste in the Hartford Metro Area. We argued that unless CE guaranteed the construction cost to complete the plant and pass a stringent commercial operation test, the state could not enhance the bonds to be issued to finance the project. The company thus finally agreed to pay for all cost overruns if need be.

In fact, there were significant cost overruns, and CE did finally pay those costs and pass the commercial operation. But these financings proved to be the catalyst for it going out of business.

The CRRA completed financing—based on the P3 model— waste-to-energy facilities in Hartford, Wallingford, Bridgeport (under a second procurement process), and Southeastern Connecticut under technologies owned by one of the two companies that could and did pass the COT.[71] A fifth was built through a locally issued bond issue in New Britain, Connecticut.

NYC Sanitation Department

Waste-to-energy failed to take hold in some places and not always for technological or financing limitations. In the 1980s, I was the partner-in-charge of counseling the NYC Sanitation Department. In that role, I was asked to draft and oversee a request for proposals (RFP) for construction and financing by a private company with technology patents in partnership with the city of a waste-to-energy facility. The solid waste tonnage generated daily in all five boroughs was enormous, so the facility not only would be a large twenty-four-hour working plant but needed to be centrally located. It had to have good roads and access for daily deliveries from sanitation trucks. Preferably, it would have water access for barging the waste to it from transfer stations located elsewhere.

Everybody involved from Mayor Ed Koch to Sanitation Commissioner Norm Steisel and his staff concluded that the Brooklyn Navy Yard was the ideal site. It was right across from downtown Wall Street with East River access and near major highways. The Navy Yard itself was large and fenced off from public view for the most part. Hence, the RFP designated it as *the* site for the plant.

The technology of this process was relatively untested. Because of that, during the RFP process, only two companies were prequalified and allowed to submit bids. They had shown that their boilers could handle solid waste burning without slagging or fouling.

One day, while doing further due diligence about the background of each of these companies, I was startled to learn that the technology's development was directly attributable to the operation of similar facilities but for different purposes—that is, the Holocaust in Germany. Within a week of my discovery, I was summoned to a meeting in the mayor's office. This time, neither I nor anyone else had a solution. A substantial Hasidic Jewish community was situated next to the Navy Yard. That community's leadership had informed Mayor Koch in no uncertain times that his incinerator to burn city garbage would not be located anywhere in Brooklyn.

To this day, city leaders have never reconsidered siting such a facility anywhere in New York City. Today, its solid waste is mostly transported to landfills in Pennsylvania, Ohio, and other states, given that the technology of properly lining landfills has finally met the stringent standards of the Environmental Protection Agency. These liner create physical barriers between the garbage and the ground to prevent leachate (liquid that drains or leaches from a landfill) and other contaminates from entering the soil and ground water. Some solid waste is also transported to the Connecticut Bridgeport waste-to-energy plant. When there is unused capacity at a price competitive with landfills, some goes to a similar plant built by the Port Authority in New Jersey.

New York City sanitation department now take a computerized bidding approach. Working with a specialized engineering firm, the department developed and coordinated a daily or weekly auction-like protocol whereby "landfill" pricing would be competitive. The department selects from bids submitted by those two waste-to-energy plants and several out-of-state approved disposal sites, including some in Pennsylvania and Ohio.

Public, Private Partnerships

The negotiations between the company with the proven technology (and clients prepared to build a waste-to-energy facility) and the county that controlled the waste flow were always arduous. Neither side had an advantage, particularly since two companies—Ogden Corporation (now Covanta) and Wheelabrator-Frye (now owned by Waste Management)—had plants operating. The community could solicit competitive bids and negotiate with the successful bidder while putting the second bidder on hold, pending the negotiations outcome.

One such negotiation occurred in Onondaga County where Ogden Corporation was the winner. Wheelabrator-Frye watched carefully to ensure the selection team kept within the bid guidelines, ready to challenge if we did not.

After two years of negotiations as the county's lead lawyer, I told the Ogden lawyers we were ready to call it quits and move to the second bidder unless we completed negotiating the remaining ten points to our satisfaction. Accordingly, Ogden's president, David Sokol, was required to be at the next meeting. In preparation for that meeting, I rearranged my list to disguise the ones that were my priority to win. I anticipated the usual "take it or leave it" session with each side winning half the points but with the company knowing the county did not want to start all over with the second bidder.

I presented my first issue and quickly David replied, "Fine. Yes, okay. What is your next point?" My next point was a tougher one for the company. We wanted it to add tougher standards to the commercial operation test. Again, David said, "Yes, okay, next." And that is how it went on all ten points. Then David said, "Okay, do we have the deal?" The county executive saw my nodding and stood to thank David. He shook his hand, saying, "We look forward to our twenty-year partnership."

Years later, I had dinner with David, who went on to become Warren Buffett's deputy and bought the most expensive home in ritzy Sarasota, Florida. I told him about my surprise that those negotiations were so successful that day. He smiled and said, "Dick, we were in our third year of developing that project. Unless we put the shovel in the ground by our fiscal year end of November, we would have had to write off all our expenses. By then, they were so high, we would have had to book a loss for my waste-to-energy division. And it's important for you to remember that signing such a twenty-year build and operations contract is just the beginning of negotiations."

This proved to be true. While these plants have been working well in every place over the years, matters constantly require renegotiation.

CHAPTER 10

Why the Patriots Didn't Move to Hartford

Public finance is exciting when a proposed project becomes the subject of daily newspaper articles. That happened on several retainers I worked on, and this chapter describes one of them involving the professional football team, the New England Patriots.

There is perhaps no better example of a public finance project that provokes more controversy and gives taxpayers more understandable political choices than a municipality's proposed siting, construction, and financing of a football or baseball stadium for a national franchise team. This is particularly true if it's being relocated to their city. That episode occurred in the New England Patriots era of the Kraft ownership before star quarterback Tom Brady came to the team.

The Kraft family owned a major manufacturing plant in Montville, Connecticut—the same town in which the Mohegan Indian nation was situated. It had established a working relationship with state officials as a result of a financing transaction with its Connecticut Development Authority. The family was well aware of Connecticut's active and aggressive interest in keeping and attracting industry with financial incentives.[72]

Robert Kraft, who lived in Brookline, Massachusetts, detested driving the county road and facing the game-day traffic congestion to Foxboro, Massachusetts, where the Patriots played. The stadium itself was considered slightly better than a high school stadium. The Massachusetts legislature wasn't being supportive of Kraft's request to finance either expanding the road or rebuilding the stadium with public funds.

In 1994, Robert Kraft had acquired the Orthwein interests in the Patriots after James Busch Orthwein's 1992 purchase from Victor Kiam, the owner of the Remington razor company, a Connecticut business. Kiam was being forced to sell from the fallout of making rude remarks about women reporters.

At one point, the well-known author Tom Clancy led a syndicate to buy the team[73] but lost out to James Orthwein. Orthwein, because of his ties to the St. Louis Busch family, was intent on moving the Boston team to St. Louis to replace the football team that had moved to Los Angeles. However, the Patriots were locked into a lease arrangement at Foxboro, and the league wouldn't let Orthwein relocate the team out of the Boston area. That resulted in Orthwein and Kraft reaching the deal they did.

Relocate the Team to Connecticut?

Connecticut's Governor John Rowland at the time was perceived as an honest and powerful governor with national political potential. He was chairman of the GOP's governors' association and awardee of the National Council of Arts for supplying state assistance to theaters in downtown Waterbury, New Haven, Hartford, and New London. He had become the ultimate political success symbol when he and the Krafts, father and son, announced in 1998 the relocation of the Patriots to an ideal site in Hartford, Connecticut.[74]

Was this a ploy by Kraft to force action by the Massachusetts legislature as many papers immediately reported? In the role of finance counsel retained by the state of Connecticut, I did not believe so, based on the facts presented in this chapter.

The proposed Hartford site intersects I-84, I-95, and I-91. These major commuting highways are relatively empty on fall Sundays or Saturdays when most NFL games are played, making it an easy turnpike drive from Kraft's home in Massachusetts. In fact, Kraft believed day-of-game drive time for him and his Massachusetts fans to Hartford would be much faster and easier than to Foxboro. It was proposed that Connecticut would build, bond, and lease for free the stadium to Kraft. To achieve that, it would count on Connecticut sales tax on day-of-game tickets and day-of-game players' income. Added to that would be souvenir and food sales tax from at least the 35,000 season ticket holders, most of whom came from Massachusetts, Rhode Island, and Maine. This would be an absolutely new revenue source for Connecticut that didn't require subtracting losses from other local attractions on game days. (Note: Massachusetts or Maine fans would unlikely be going to movie venues in Connecticut, even if they chose not to attend the game.)

Because Kraft's team at the time didn't sell out all the seats at Foxboro, it was losing TV money due to the NFL blackout policy. (That meant if tickets for that day's game were not sold out, the TV for that area was blacked out to encourage ticket sales.) Under that NFL policy, if the Patriots played in Hartford, the Boston TV market would be available and not blacked out regardless of the Hartford attendance.[75] Given that, it was a perfect, provable economic fit for both the state of Connecticut and Kraft.

Further, the Krafts brought the promise of further economic activity by relocating the practice facility to Hartford as well. Plus the prestige of hosting an NFL team was a political winner, even if its prospects of winning championships were speculative in that pre-Brady period.

Bonding Legislation Passed

Hawkins was retained to draft the bonding legislation that was passed almost unanimously without alteration. Along with a Hartford law firm led by Scott Murphy, we began detailed lease negotiations. I, of course, was at the ready on force majeure, construction delay, insurance, and other lease build-finance provisions because of my expertise in drafting and negotiating waste-to-energy projects as discussed in a prior chapter. Scott and I just needed to beef up the sections on advertising, ticket, and other sales unique to a day-of-game enterprise. Counsel for the Patriots pushed not only for a quick negotiation but a fair one. Skybox rights, season ticket rights, and advertising details were all open to profit sharing after the Patriots' owners achieved a certain profit level. The expected options on the Connecticut location for a practice facility were included as well, bringing more state income taxes from players and personnel as well as additional publicity from preseason action.

For the governor, the stadium site selected had been a simple choice because in the previous year of 1997, the well-respected chairman of Phoenix Insurance Company, Bob Fiondella, had publicly announced a shopping and housing development of the site next to its headquarters.[76]

Unforeseen Hurdles

As negotiations commenced, the Hartford law firm proceeded to work on securing the site. The Krafts had been promised a fast-track negotiation and construction period. Finishing the stadium two to three years from the start seemed reasonable. But as we discovered more about the existing owners of the site, it became clear we couldn't meet that schedule. Not only that, but state condemnation and the vicissitudes of the prices in acquiring the site would be costly and time consuming. Why? The land did not have a sole owner.

For Governor Rowland, it was a logical assumption that Phoenix Insurance Company had secured the rights to the site. After all, what corporate executive announces a major all-purpose development of a site under which the ownership isn't clear? (Later on, many questioned the business acumen of Fiondella in announcing such a development before securing the rights to the site for doing it.[77])

Some commentary blames one of the parcel owners, the steam company, for "haggling" on the price, but that is unfair to the executives of a private company with stockholders.[78] One parcel was owned by a publicly traded cement company whose facility would have to be relocated. Another parcel was owned by the Hartford pension fund that acquired the negotiating leverage of the site being selected for this prosperous and prominent business. And a third site had title confusion as to who actually owned it. Suffice it to say getting title or even the leasehold property enough to start and complete on the time schedule or even with a reasonable year or two extension was problematic.

Another major hurdle equally as insurmountable as acquiring title to the site was that the NFL Commissioner, Paul Tagliabue, publicly opposed the move to Hartford. The commissioner I understood aggressively pursued powerful forces in the Catholic Church in Massachusetts to use its leverage with the Massachusetts legislature. He pushed for legislation to expand and pay for the road to and from the stadium in Foxboro. This would make Kraft happy to keep the team in his home state. He not only lobbied to keep the team in Foxboro, but he proposed a participation loan by the NFL as an incentive.

Kraft Caves

When the complexity acquiring the site became public and the Massachusetts legislature did as the Catholic Church wanted,[79] Kraft caved. Governor Rowland accepted the result and let the newspapers claim he had been "used" as a negotiating tactic by the wily Kraft. In my view, that was not Kraft's motivation. He truly was planning to move; he'd had it with this kind of influence in Boston. He also liked the way Connecticut had treated his son in a Montville plant prior to financing the deal.

At the beginning of negotiations, my own due diligence was an evening of cocktailing with Kraft (senior and junior) reminiscing about my schooling in West Newton and Andover and my work as bond counsel to the Connecticut Development Authority on their Montville plant financing. They had convinced me of their sincerity in the move, particularly because we discussed the logical place for a practice facility.

Speaker of the House Tom Ritter, who had shepherded through the legislation, was also convinced of the sincerity of the Krafts, knowing that senior Kraft had started looking for a home to buy in West Hartford. What I learned later solved the mystery about Tagliabue's antagonism to Connecticut. It later became public that the NFL had settled a multimillion-dollar antitrust case brought on by Orthwein that was still pending and in negotiations at the time Kraft was moving to Connecticut. He had claimed treble damages because the NFL had required a second round of bidding on the sale of the Patriots by Kiam that prevented him from winning and moving the team to St. Louis. It became clear that if the NFL had allowed the Patriots to move to Hartford, it would have proven to be an arbitrary decision by the NFL to prevent Orthwein's move to St. Louis.[80] Hartford, like St. Louis, was a different TV market, so despite being in New England, there was no rational business purpose in preventing the team from moving to St. Louis and not preventing it from moving to Hartford.

PART THREE

Creativity in Public Finance

CHAPTER 11

What Is
NYC Water Authority?

The public finance practice is most rewarding when structuring a financing that provides the municipality with a much-needed infrastructure. This chapter explains what happened when New York City's Port Authority asked me for "thinking" time.

Can you imagine how, for the entire twentieth century, two water tunnels built in the nineteenth century served the growing New York City population? The third water tunnel, under construction for the past sixty years by sandhogs (underground construction workers), is as large as a 747 airplane's wingspan.

In 1986, I received the most unusual call of my fifty-some-year career. General Counsel Jeff Greene of the Port Authority of New York and New Jersey offered me a fee of $75,000 to "think" how to structure a water authority for the city of New York similar to the Buffalo Sewer Authority. The city of Buffalo and the Port Authority had, under different retainers, requested Chester Johnson of Government Finance Associates, a highly regarded financial advisory firm, to pursue, respectively, the feasibility of a water authority for the city of Buffalo and the city of New York.

At that time, my firm (with me as partner-in-charge) was bond counsel for the city of Buffalo as well as the Buffalo Sewer Authority, so Chester knew my expertise in this area. I told him and Buffalo's city attorney and comptroller that replicating the structure of the Buffalo Sewer Authority was not legally possible. There was an explicit constitutional provision, Article 10-5, that had been added as an amendment to the New York Constitution to preclude that from happening in other cities. But why? Here's the background story.

When Buffalo's mayor was defeated running for another term in 1938, he caused the state legislature to create the Buffalo Sewer Authority. Then he shifted his political cronies to become its employees. The Buffalo Sewer Authority would own and manage the city's sewer system and therefore be insulated from being fired by the new incoming mayor. That authority was created, assigned ownership of the sewer system, and from 1935 onward, issued bonds to finance improvements and established rates and charges to pay for debt service on their bonds. It would also pay for all employees who maintained and operated the sewage disposal facility as well as the interceptors, laterals, and sewer mains of the system. In effect, every employee benefitted from the Democratic patronizing system.

It so happened that, at the time of creating the Buffalo Sewer Authority and its resulting publicity, the voices of good government were being heard in Albany. The state legislature was then debating in convened sessions on revisions to the New York State Constitution. Good-governance voices screamed that it should never again be possible to set up such a sanctuary for political patronage as the Buffalo Sewer Authority. As a result, Article 10-5 was added to the Constitution. It reads as follows:

No such public corporation shall hereafter be given both the power to contract indebtedness and the power, within any city, to collect rentals, charges, rates or fees from the owners of real estate, or the occupants of real estate . . . for services or facilities furnished or supplied in connection with such real estate, if such services or facilities are of a character or nature then or formerly furnished or supplied by the city, unless the electors of the city shall approve the granting to such corporation of such powers by a majority vote at a general or special election in such city . . .[81]

It was easy for me to counsel the city that a new water authority had no chance of being created except by either a constitutional amendment or an approving referendum, given the straightforward prohibitive language of this section of the law and, neither of these was politically realistic.

However, my friend Chester Johnson[82] claimed he heard hesitation or doubt in my counseling. So unbeknown to me, he told Jeff Greene he thought I might find a way to "think" about how to do it by just a statutory amendment. Jeff noted the Port Authority's interest: bonds secured by water rates were needed to finance the cost of further construction and completion of the third water tunnel into New York City. The great watershed of New York was at risk, and the city government had requested the Port Authority look into the matter. The construction of the third water terminal was already underway in New York City. As a result of years of delay due to the 1975 fiscal crisis, the cost had hugely increased. That meant city leaders had to find a new revenue resource. There was simply no way general taxes could continue to support the debt services on the additional bonds needed to finance the tunnel's completion.

By creating a water authority to finance the remaining completion cost and thereafter assure the water system would be maintained in good repair, they believed the use of water could be metered and users charged for what they consumed. That kind of revenue resource was standard in many states. Definitely, it would relieve the general fund real estate levy as the source for debt service and operation and maintenance of the water system. Those were the facts.

My Constitutional Interpretation

With that constitutional restriction and those facts in mind, I wrote a constitutional interpretation consistent with the leading case in the New York Court of Appeals by Chief Justice Breitel. I used the precise wording of that constitutional amendment and created a new security structure that proved to be well received by the bond market. In New York, in a key case, the highest court had upheld legislation-creating authorities if the Act did not "patently violate" the letter of law.[83] Thus, structuring legislation to purposely circumvent a constitutional provision needed precision, but a court would likely uphold it if the wording did not "patently" contradict that provision.

Meanwhile, public interest groups at the time fully supported metering water as a revenue resource. It was accepted that consumers would use less water if it directly cost them money for usage. Also, it would be politically popular to impose different rates and charges for commercial and residential use. Moreover, this sensible economic and bond market motivation was not an effort to protect power in a patronage package; thus, the primary underlying purpose of the constitutional amendment was not being circumvented.

Solving the Problem

Here was my solution: One, the wording of my legislation created an authority to issue bonds; two, it created a totally separate water board entity to establish the proper rates and charges; three, it would leave the city government with the power to continue operating and maintaining the water system, including awarding all contracts and hiring employees. This trifurcation—the functions of a contracting indebtedness, charging and collecting rates, and operating—was a perfect fit that explicitly did not violate Article 10-5.

This solution would comply with that provision of the constitution. It prohibited an authority with the power to both issue bonds *and* charge rates while operating a function formerly provided by a city. To be confident it would be upheld by a court challenge, I drafted a clause that no city official could be appointed to either the newly formed authority or the water board, including both the mayor or the city comptroller (ex officio or otherwise). This would insulate it from a challenge on either substance or form since both bonding authority and the rate-making board were independent of the city officials who would continue to operate the water system. Truly a trifurcation in form and substance.

I drafted that legislation and sent it over to Jeff Greene, including a detailed letter stating its theory. I also stated that if passed exactly as drafted, Hawkins would render an affirming validity opinion on its constitutionality. Jeff thanked me, and we had a long conversation about why I thought the trifurcation would work not only to legally circumvent the constitutional amendment but would also be welcomed by the financial community of financial advisors, investment bankers, and bond buyers. Having an independent rate-making function was a new feature for a public authority. Over the years, this aspect became highly regarded by both the rating agencies and bond investors for insulating that function from political influences.

One Irate Comptroller

Shortly after my proposal and letter to Jeff Greene were delivered, I was in a client meeting on the twelfth floor when my assistant interrupted to inform me Harrison (Jay) Goldin, the city comptroller, was on the phone. I said to tell him I'd take the call in my office on the thirteenth floor. As I remember the call, without a return of my hello, I heard one irate city comptroller demand to know "how in hell" I could draft any new board involved in any city enterprise without his office not being on the board—and not chairing that board—particularly when it's a bonding authority or rate-making board. No, Goldin declared he had *not* needed to read my letter accompanying the legislation. Then I alluded to the constitutional provision (Article 10-5) around which I was crafting a structure, that I was retained to draft an acceptable valid structure for that purpose and so that my firm could render an unqualified opinion upon the issuance of the bonds.

I suggested he call other counsel to assist him. But in no way could I support his request to change the legislation that would put his office (in fact or ex officio) on either board. I added that, given his position as city comptroller with or without specific membership on a board, he would always have controlling influence in selecting the bond underwriters and other consultants for both the financing authority and the rate-making board. Goldin stated he would be talking to other counsel and, without a goodbye, slammed down the phone.

Later that week, I took a call from my friend and partner at Rogers & Wells, the then bond counsel for the city. He said that he and his firm not only had reviewed putting the city comptroller on the board of the two entities, but after researching it, concluded my trifurcation theory was interesting. However, his firm was not prepared to render a marketable opinion on the structure.

Hawkins Not Retained

The legislation was enacted, all appointments were made, and all consultants were picked. My firm, Hawkins, was not retained for any role. At another meeting with Mayor Koch, my partners Donald Robinson, John Connorton, and I were cornered by the comptroller, who made a point of mentioning he did have the influence to assure Hawkins would not be retained.

After successfully selling about a billion dollars of bonds and imposing the water rates on consumers, a lawsuit was filed by several Queens legislators challenging the constitutionality of this legislation. The chair of the new water board retained our firm, knowing we had the research ready to go to defend its constitutionality. Because billions of bonds had already been issued and invalidation would create a fiscal crisis for the city, the comptroller did not stop that retainer. I had the cumbersome task of convincing my litigation partner, Cullen MacDonald, how the trifurcation theory worked. I provided him with supporting cases and wrote the defense answer to my satisfaction.

Finally, the day arrived when the case was scheduled for oral arguments in the Supreme Court, which is the lower court in New York, in the courtroom of Judge Eve Preminger (a niece of the famous movie producer Otto Preminger). In the oral argument, Judge Preminger questioned why the same legislators who sponsored the legislation were now challenging it. Their counsel responded by saying they did not understand that meters would be imposed on the homes of their constituents and had not been aware of the constitutional prohibition creating such an authority. The judge then extensively questioned the counsel about the relationship of the water board and the authority to the comptroller. Yes, each were "renting" space in the comptroller's office at City Hall, but no, the city comptroller had no role, official or unofficial, on either board. This was a clear signal of support for my concern and a rebuke to the city comptroller.

The judge concluded the oral argument by stating that if all counsel would wait, she had to add a paragraph to her opinion, which would be ready in twenty minutes. The opinion upheld the legislation[84] and specifically noted in that added paragraph that no city official was on the authority or the rate board as the crucial fact of why the legislation did not conflict with the constitutional amendment.[85]

As a result, the bonds of the authority have been rated triple A, the water tunnel has been completed, and the concept of separating the bonding authority from the rate-making power has been replicated for situations in which structuring around a constitutional restriction was not even necessary. I have never been thanked by Mr. Goldin for my refusal to honor his request.

CHAPTER 12

What Is a
Secured Repo?

*This chapter recounts my introduction to the bankruptcy
risks inherent in structuring public finance bond issues.
It reflects an inside story of working with one of the most
delightful mayors of NYC. Mayor Ed Koch entertained
the taxpayers of the city for twelve years yet is not noted
for any major accomplishments. Given the number of
elected officials being convicted of criminal activity or
resigning on improper sexual proclivities, to his credit,
Mayor Koch is noted for not having any corrupt activities
or misadventures.*

On August 13, 1982, Wall Street woke up to a financial disaster.
That's when the repurchase multibillion-dollar borrowing market
(REPOs) fell apart with the bankruptcy filing of Lombard-Wall, Inc.,
listing debts of $177.2 million to unsecured creditors.[86]

REPOs are usually short-term borrowings, lasting from overnight to thirty days. A dealer sells government securities (think U.S. Treasuries) to investors and agrees to repurchase them on the specified short-term date.

On August 14, I received a call from my assistant, Jeanne Carlson, while in a meeting at the midtown office of Debevoise Plimpton. We were talking about financing the first so-called public-private partnership by Wheelabrator-Frye of a waste-to-energy incinerator to burn solid waste. Jeanne said she knew I didn't want to be interrupted, but David Brown, deputy mayor to Mayor Ed Koch and partner at Hawkins the previous year, demanded to talk to me.

David told me to be in Mayor Koch's office in the next fifteen minutes. It involved the Lombard-Wall bankruptcy[87] filing and "your client," New York City Housing Development Corporation (HDC). The HDC president had informed Mayor Koch that it had close to $130 million of its bond proceeds invested in REPOs. The "your client" inflection in his voice immediately put me on guard. Then I recalled hearing on the news the night before about the bankruptcy of Lombard-Wall.

Before I left Debevoise, I called Hawkins' bankruptcy associate, Olivia O'Neill, to join me at City Hall. I told her not to go into the mayor's office until I arrived. She had not worked on the facts of the documentation prepared by me for HDC on its REPOs transaction with Lombard-Wall. The mayor's office was large enough to accommodate more than twenty people—all wearing dark suits and ties for the men and dark suits for the three women—that included lawyers and clients who were already seated. Two folding chairs were brought in for Olivia and me, and I moved them close to Michael C. Smith, president of HDC.

The mayor and his corporation counsel were already grilling a lawyer representing one of the other city-affiliated entities, New York State Dormitory Authority, on the facts and circumstances as well as the estimated loss for his client. That lawyer, Scott Sykes, was a good friend and a partner at Sykes, Galloway & Dikeman (SG&D), where his father was a founding partner.

The New York State Dormitory Authority, a New York public benefit general corporation, was established to issue tax-exempt bonds to finance dormitories of state-owned or city-owned universities. Then (and even in recent years), it had become the largest bond issuer in New York for assorted capital infrastructure purposes and projects primarily promoting the particular agenda of the governor in office. No statewide bond referendum was required to authorize these projects, so it was (and still is) a conduit issuer for financing various projects for the state or city.

The REPO documentation of that New York State Dormitory Authority's REPO transaction (as explained by that partner) would classify that Authority as a general "unsecured" creditor in the bankruptcy court proceeding. The partners nervously acknowledged that the Authority could expect to incur the entire REPOs loss of $55 million. In fact, the Authority did incur the full $55 million loss, and as a consequence, SG&D lost it as a client. SG&D had been its exclusive bond counsel since its inception in the late 1940s, and Scott left his firm and moved to Texas where he later practiced healthcare law.

After the Dormitory Authority, Mayor Koch "demanded" a review of facts about HDC's arrangements with Lombard-Wall. Mike Smith deferred to me as his counsel. Without hesitation, I stated I was bond counsel for HDC and that the REPOs transaction between Lombard and HDC was the subject of a written security agreement. I also said that, lodged in trust with U.S. Trust was an amount of U.S. Treasuries equal to the REPOs. I added that my bankruptcy specialist Ms. O'Neill had told me there would be a "stay and delay" for the court to review those documents. However, upon such a security review, those U.S. Treasuries would be released free and clear to HDC. Accordingly, HDC would suffer no loss.

This surprised Mayor Koch, as evidenced by the broad smile on his face as that "good news" sunk in. Those seated around the room reacted in shock as they began to understand and appreciate my analysis. It seemed that I had invented "secured" REPOs.[88]

HDC continues to be a Hawkins client exclusively. It issues bonds prolifically every year for low- and moderate-income housing developments. After that event, Hawkins also became one of the few law firms to represent the Dormitory Authority.

Result of Research

Why had I prepared such secured transaction documents and counseled the client that security be transferred and lodged with a separate bank? This came directly as the result of research back in the late 1960s done at the request of a Hawkins partner, Gerry Fernandez, for his client Franklin National Bank—a general service bank with many branches on Long Island.

The leaders at Franklin National Bank asked if compliance with the New York Local Finance Law, which required public deposits in a bank to be secured by U.S. Treasuries, could be secured by lodging those treasuries with the trust department of the same bank. My memo was based on listening to and learning from Soia Mentschikoff, my University of Chicago law school professor. Also my moot court mentor, Soia had taught Chapter 9 of the Uniform Commercial Code, Secured Transactions, which she and her husband Professor Karl Llewelyn had drafted. Soia had summarized it this way: "Collateral to be secure in a bankruptcy proceeding had to be out of the possession of the entity that promised to repay. Hence, it was clear to me the trust department of the same bank in which the money was deposited did not meet that test. I could not track down any legal precedent supporting the so-called 'Chinese wall' between the two bank departments."[89]

In a memorandum of law addressed to partner Fernandez, I stated that the client be instructed that the best practice was to have another bank hold the treasuries in escrow. Gerry had given that memo (labeled by him as "preliminary") to the bank officer who requested our counsel.

That "preliminary" addition was meant to preclude the advice to be actual and final, anticipating the bank officer would want to have further discussions and maybe suggest alternatives. That was the last request for legal services from that client.

I do not think Gerry ever sent the bank a bill, as it clearly was not the answer the bank wanted. For all I know, banks with trust departments continue with the same "culture" of "securing" public deposits by paper credit allocation to their respective trust departments. Such practice is commonly thought to be protected by the Chinese wall defense.

Became My Beacon

That early bank question was my first experience with the bankruptcy law. It became my beacon with respect to the range of securing contract transactions under the light of that law. Thus I had drafted documents requiring Lombard-Wall to lodge the equivalent amount of securities in trust in another institution. As for my 1966 assignment, Gerry had originally thought Franklin could become the source of significant fees for the firm, particularly as it had just opened its first branch in Manhattan in our Wall Street area. But that memo did us in.

However, that bank later came under the control of unsavory owners and was declared insolvent. Its officers were convicted of fraud, extradited, and lodged in an Italian prison under mysterious circumstances.[90] Also, of ironic interest, Harold Kurtz was the bank officer that Gerry had been cultivating at Franklin Bank in 1966. He had moved on to be president of Lombard-Wall and was there when the company filed for bankruptcy in 1982.

When I first entered the meeting in the mayor's office, I was able to greet Deputy Mayor David Brown on a first-name basis as my former partner. Not only that, Mayor Koch also recognized me by first name, as I had been appointed and presented by him at a press conference early in his administration as one of several "$1 per year deputy mayors." I would provide advice on the disposal of solid waste by the city and financing of waste-to-energy facilities.

After that, Mayor Koch had seen me working with intensity. In fact, before this meeting, I had been offered the official full-time position of deputy mayor for economic development by David Brown at the urging of the mayor. I was perfectly qualified for the position; I had been bond counsel for the state of Connecticut on many general obligation and revenue bond issues. I had also drafted the statute creating a statewide finance authority for the construction of several waste-to-energy plants to produce over 25 percent of the electricity needed by the companies in that state. In addition, I had drafted the statute creating (and been bond counsel on many issues for) the Connecticut Development Authority to provide tax-exempt financing for companies seeking to move to Connecticut. The financing was to build facilities, or, if already in Connecticut, to build bigger in-state facilities.

These two retainers were the beginning of what's become a booming bond financing practice of putting government together with private companies in a mutually beneficial business public-private partnership. That offer to join the Koch Administration as deputy mayor intrigued me because of both the public service honor and the wonderful opportunity to work for such a personality.

Stayed with Hawkins

Despite my qualifications and interest, I apologized to David when I rejected this offer. I said I didn't have the patience for working within the city administration. The mayor has to deal with so many diverse matters needing policy decisions that no one deputy's agenda could be fast tracked. I realized I could do better for the city as its finance counsel on certain matters such as economic development and solid waste disposal while also working on bond issues for other clients. After that, Hawkins (yours truly) was retained for hourly pay to counsel the city's sanitation development leaders on alternative ways to dispose of solid waste. Hawkins continues in that role to this day; it has developed a detailed daily "auction" protocol for disposal of its solid waste at out-of-state landfills.

Similarly, Hawkins has been retained as the bond counsel to the New York City Industrial Development Agency on many small bond issues. That entity is a conduit tax-exempt financing agency for small private companies to finance and construct manufacturing and other commercial facilities within the volume amount capped by the Internal Revenue Code Section 103 restrictions.[91] Of course, Hawkins was also still serving as bond counsel to the Municipal Assistance Corporation for the City of New York. Later, I collaborated with my long-standing investment banker friend, Joe Lhota, when he was serving the Giuliani administration. We developed the first state-based securitization program in New York, the Transitional Finance Authority, which has become a key structure for financing capital improvements for the city.

One other factor gave me pause about working for this mayor. At one point—on a matter of solid waste policy, work shifts, and manning of trucks—the mayor invited me to participate in two back-to-back meetings with two dissimilar groups of constituents. They included residents of large apartment buildings along Park Avenue in Manhattan as well as buildings in the other boroughs (for one) and representative union officials for garbage truck drivers' and helpers' union officials (for the other). The meetings, held around ten a.m. for two hours on two consecutive days, discussed the hours for pickup, traffic congestion, noise control, and other issues at the core of city living.

Each meeting had about fifteen constituents in attendance in addition to the mayor, two of his aides, and me. I took extensive notes and Mayor Koch participated. Each attendee had his or her say, and an active repartee with the mayor followed. The meetings ended with each group thinking participants had not only had a full airing of issues, but they had concluded a deal with the mayor, resulting in smiles all around. However, after reviewing my notes and conferring with his aides, we came to a strange conclusion: that agreement on the issues discussed on the second day was almost exactly the opposite of the agreement on the same issues discussed the first day. Mayor Koch loved the dialogue but was not an ideologue; he did not want to have a meeting end in disagreement—classic Koch.

Today, when I look back on his administration, I appreciate it as a great three-term popular run, but it's unclear what was accomplished in the years under Mayor Koch.

Secure Financing

The Lombard-Wall finance structure was the first of many financings in which I was faced with anticipating the result of what was (or was not) a secure financing. This was in the event my client, a governmental body such as a public authority or municipality or its corporate partner on a public-private project financing, resorted to filing for bankruptcy.

In 1969, I called Professor Soia Mentschikoff, my mentor at the University of Chicago Law School, when I had a concern regarding two clients. One was a university that was issuing dormitory bonds to be secured by tuition fees; the other was a turnpike authority issuing bonds to be secured by tolls collected at toll booths. I asked her how to secure the payment of the tuition fees at the university's bursar office and the tolls collected at the toll booth. She politely told me that I missed the most obvious point of secured transactions—that possession is everything and cash is king. The amount cannot be secured until it is deposited, in trust, in a bank trust account. Therefore, during the collection period and while the money is in the bursar's office or in the cash box at the toll booth, it is not secured.

I counseled each client that an unsecured risk existed. The only option was to hire and put an employee of the bank trustee appointed under the bond indenture to work in the bursar's office or toll booth (each technically doable but totally impractical). The result was to draft a covenant requiring daily deposits into a nearby trust account of the bank. This would minimize the loss if the issuer did file for bankruptcy.

Of course, based on that "technical" day of being unsecured, we had to revise our disclosure and opinion documents to reference the exception of the pledge. Before then, it stated the bonds were validly issued and the tuition fees/tolls validly pledged (without any exception).

An Early Blunder

Despite not being a partner at Hawkins, sometime in 1968 I was included in a special meeting of partners and select associates. At this meeting, Henry Miller was proposing to become our partner and bring his burgeoning bankruptcy practice to the firm. Bear in mind none of the blue chip corporate firms had a bankruptcy practice in the 1960s or early 1970s. The similar practice of defending corporate executives accused of "white collar" crime was also not considered worthy of practice by established blue chip Wall Street corporate firms.

Henry proposed leveraging our firm's well-regarded special municipal finance bond practice and our impeccable reputation with Wall Street brokerage firms to attract corporate clients considering bankruptcy. Theoretically, large firms having many corporate clients would recommend Hawkins because we would not be a threat to take over their corporate clients after emerging from a bankruptcy restructuring proceeding.

Unfortunately, we believed that having a bankruptcy practice was an embarrassment. This move would damage our bond business by representing corporate clients wanting to default on their debt obligations by filing for bankruptcy. Can you imagine the opportunity we missed? But we weren't alone. Most prestigious firms held the same view of that practice in the pre-Drexel/Milken/Texaco/Lehman Brothers/ General Motors/Enron period.

Fast forward to 1969 when Henry Miller became the fourteenth partner in Weil, Gotshal & Manges, a firm that thereafter thrived on corporate bankruptcies. At Henry's death in 2015, his firm of more than one thousand lawyers proudly stated this:

Miller was the leading force in the evolution of Weil into one of the world's predominate law firms and is responsible for making the bankruptcy, restructuring and reorganization practice an integral practice group of most major law firms.[92]

Great foresight is credited to Ira Milstein, Weil's managing partner for years, who, in 1969, recognized that kind of practice for its potential and brought Henry on board. Milstein won the daily double for his firm when he hired John R. Wing as a partner and as a white collar criminal defense attorney. Wing had established a stellar prosecuting attorney reputation as chief of frauds at the United States Attorney's office. Thus that firm was ready to roll when other rich Wall Street folks were indicted and needed to be defended.

In retrospect, I made the right decision in turning down Koch's offer to be deputy mayor, as my *non sibi* for the city was my service in developing several new programs for its benefit. However, I clearly missed out in expanding my firm as we turned down Miller and his bankruptcy practice. It had never occurred to me to ask Mr. Wing, my law school roommate, to become my partner and start a "white collar crime" practice at my firm.

CHAPTER 13

What Are the Fundamentals of Public Finance?

This chapter highlights my early years as a municipal bond finance attorney at a Wall Street law firm. It also provides a basic tutorial of state and local governmental public finance through examples from the state of Alaska.

I became a public finance lawyer by lucky chance. In 1963, Louis Auchincloss, a recognized author of fiction about practicing law and serving wealthy New York clients, was a managing partner at Hawkins, Delafield & Wood. He had posted notice on the New York University Law School bulletin board of an opening at his firm. The New York University Law School library, which sits across the street from Washington Square Park, is a temporary home to many would-be lawyers from out-of-city law schools studying for the New York State bar exam.[93] I thought it would be interesting to interview with him, especially as his firm had an actual Wall Street address.

I found Mr. Auchincloss to be charming with that affluent Upper East Side dialect.[94] He offered me a position starting in "bonds." When I asked him about specializing in bonds, he shrugged and said that Hawkins was good in that specialty and had an opening.

Hawkins had been established in 1864. In the 1960s, it was considered a well-regarded full-service firm with banking, litigation, corporate, trusts, and estates practices. It also had a unique specialty, representing state and local issuers of tax-exempt municipal bonds as their bond counsel. I accepted his offer, and on April 4, 1964, I started there as an associate—the eighth associate in a firm of fifteen partners. The ratio and size seemed ideal to make partnership (the basic goal of 1960s law graduates) compared to my University of Chicago Law School classmates. They had started at Shearman & Sterling; Willkie, Farr; and Weil, Gotshal with ratios of three to four associates per partner and *more than one hundred lawyers.*

Today, the legal profession has become a multifaceted, worldwide business with consolidation of law firms throughout the United States and the world. Partners are making regular moves from one firm to another, a trajectory course that's now anticipated for starting attorneys at these "Wall Street" firms.

Following a Basic Formula

As I quickly learned in the early years of my practice, the issuance of bonds followed a basic formula. An issuer would be a state, public authority, or municipality. Before processing a bond issue, the issuer would hire Hawkins to represent it and visit the rating agency that would rate the creditworthiness of the bond. Hawkins would draft the bond and disclosure documents, then provide at the closing the so-called approving opinion, respecting the validity of the bonds and their interest exemption from state, local, and federal income taxes. Often, we'd end up at the printers the day before a mailing to ensure the offering statements were properly complete. The bonds, in coupon form, were manually signed by the chief fiscal officer at the Signature Company the day of closing. Very few firms had this public financing specialty that focused on federal, state, and local laws relevant to the bond procedures and tax exemption.

While many Wall Street law firms and banking institutions moved to midtown Manhattan from 1960 to 1980, Hawkins remained downtown. This was primarily because the Signature Company had a unique machine of one pen orchestrating ten pens, allowing racking and signing of bonds simultaneously. And it remained downtown.

Signing and delivering the executed bonds to the underwriters in New York meant government officials from Alaska, Hawaii, California, and all other states came east to "close" the bond financing in New York. This was considered a required perk by those officials. In addition, the major rating agencies, Moody's, Standard & Poors, and then-upstart Fitch, were also downtown, which allowed governmental officials to meet with each rating agency. The personal rapport during these visits with the clients cannot be undervalued. A featured conversation at the closing dinner usually brought about the next significant deal.

The Hawkins firm is called a "national" practice in that any state and municipality or any governmental financing authority could retain the firm on its bond issue. Having the firm's approving opinion on those bonds is now and was then accepted by the national banks and institutional underwriters. Most were originally headquartered in New York, but today, they're found in any money market U.S. city. Our firm did not physically expand to other states (as other firms had done) until the 1980s. Then, certain state clients such as California, Connecticut, and New Jersey commanded we open an in-state office by threatening to retain "local" firms to approve their bond issues.

Great Alaskan Earthquake and Resulting Bonds Required

The Great Alaskan earthquake[95] occurred on Good Friday, March 27, 1964, just a few days before I started at Hawkins. Three months later —on the Wednesday before the July 4th weekend—I was walking back from lunch. While walking down Wall Street, I noticed and greeted John Brubaker, a friend and fellow lacrosse midfielder from prep school (Andover) and college (Yale). John was sitting on the steps of the Federal Hall,[96] which was on Wall Street across from the New York Exchange and the J. P. Morgan headquarters.[97] He told me that, as the assistant attorney general for Alaska, he was waiting for his two p.m. appointment with a senior finance partner of a Wall Street firm. (Please see Appendix C for background information on how Wall Street once operated and how it has changed since 1964.)

John had been enticed to take the position of Alaska's assistant attorney general because of its high salary of $9,000 a year (compared to Wall Street's going rate in 1964 of $7,800) to practice in that state. He also wanted to break out of the Eastern preppy mold. His assignment was to retain a Mr. Russell, reportedly the best bond lawyer in the nation and to request the firm's legal opinion approving the bond financing proffered by the state and necessitated by the devastation of downtown Anchorage by the earthquake.

I told him Mr. Russell was a partner in the firm I had just joined. Although I had yet to meet him, I said I'd be pleased to show him the way to the firm farther west at 67 Wall Street. As we walked, I told John that Mr. Auchincloss said I'd start with bonds at a starting salary of $7,500, because government retainers were not as "rich" as corporate retainers. He also said I had the benefit of working for the public good and not just for profit-motivated corporations.

It didn't hurt to mention that both Louis Auchincloss and Ike Russell were also Yale graduates.

We went up to Mr. Russell's four-window corner office. There, I asked him if I could introduce my classmate whom I'd just met on Wall Street. Mr. Russell said, "Come in and sit down. I need your help. My associate, Eric Wohlforth, is on vacation this month." That was the start of my mentoring by Ike Russell and the beginning of a retainer of the firm by the state of Alaska, which continues today.

Ike Russell Accomplishments

Ike Russell is credited with suggesting the use of the rock excavations for the original two World Trade Center Towers be used to expand Manhattan Island. Instead of being barged to New Jersey landfills, that rubble would form what is now known as Battery Park City. Mr. Russell then drafted the lease of the vast landfill extension by New York City to the Battery Park City Authority. This was part of our retainer as the bond counsel for the bond issue that built the first of many new structures.

Ike had been editor-in-chief of the *Yale Law Review* and, with another partner, Arnold Frye, he was also known for saving the state of New Jersey and many of its municipalities from defaulting on debt in the 1930s. How? By arranging "shotgun" refundings (exchange of outstanding bonds for new bonds with deferred payment of principal) between bondholders and those issuers with higher interest rates.

In the 1960s, he was called "Mr. Turnpike" for crafting the first revenue tolling bond indentures for Maine, New Hampshire, Connecticut, and New Jersey Turnpike Authority issuers, as well as for the Delaware Bridge Authority bond indenture.

Bonds for Rebuilding Alaska

The bond proposal that John brought to Mr. Russell on behalf of Alaska raised a formidable first-impression question. Upon its statehood in 1959, Alaska had adopted a standard state constitutional provision prohibiting the issuance of general obligation bonds by the state without prior approval. That meant a majority of its citizens had to vote for it at a referendum, *except when dealing with a natural emergency* or military invasion.

The 1964 earthquake devastated an area (among other places) of large, new, expensive private homes in the most exclusive area of downtown Anchorage. Houses were leveled and, being on the fault line of that earthquake, any rebuilding on the entire area was precluded. Consequently, that area today is simply a wide, elongated greenway.

Homeowners—typical of most who ventured to Anchorage in the days of early development—used mortgages to finance building new homes and then—also typical in Alaska when major downturns in luck occurred—left the state. By doing so, they abandoned any effort to repay the mortgages without worrying about debt collectors or credit score companies finding them in the lower forty-eight states.

In the 1960s, due diligence for traditional lending required onsite personnel. Yet in the remote state of Alaska, there was neither enough business to warrant locating bank offices there nor enough qualified lending officers willing to move far away without a high salary to entice them. As a result, the only major bank willing to make home mortgages in Alaska had been the Bowery Savings Bank of New York. The state had determined that, to enhance its reputation for protecting companies invested in Alaska to foster investment in the state, it had to rescue the bank from the earthquake-related mortgage losses by paying off the mortgages in full on those high-end homes.

The state also realized that a referendum to approve the bond issue would be unpopular. Indeed, it would be soundly defeated as a bailout of a New York bank and the absconding homeowners. Under those circumstances, John asked Mr. Russell whether financing could proceed without a vote based on that exception of "meeting a natural emergency." An essential principle for any state bond issue, he asked, "Is such a financing serving a proper public purpose?" If yes, it meant the entire population in Alaska would need to be taxed to repay the debt service on bonds that arguably benefited only a few individuals (i.e., for a private purpose).[98] Mr. Russell and I thanked John for retaining us and began to research these questions.

I then had to call my fiancée of only two weeks and say we had to postpone our trip to Buffalo for me to meet her parents. Researching this issue had become my July 4th weekend priority. By late Monday, I had researched every case in every state on exceptions to referendum requirements, and I concluded there was no controlling precedent (for or against). The Alaska facts simply were not squarely within the precedents, which involved financing soup kitchens, road repairs, debris removal, or extraordinary expenses resulting from hurricanes, tornadoes, or floods.

Given such facts, I proposed that we "test" litigate[99] because I anticipated the court would uphold a bond statute that properly presented the facts and legislative findings. I thought it would also uphold the bond issue as appropriate, modern-day financial disaster relief occasioned by the natural earthquake. However, without such an approving judicial opinion, we could not provide our unqualified approving opinion concerning the bond issue's validity to the purchasers of the bonds.

At the time, bond counsel was expected to render validity opinions only if there was not a scintilla of a doubt about the outcome of a challenge to validity. That is the so-called summary judgment standard. In effect, that means the facts are established without dispute. The law is sufficiently settled by precedents that no trial would be necessary for a judge to render a favorable summary judgment on a complaint challenging the validity of the bond issue.

Suber v. Alaska Test Case

Mr. Russell and Mr. Brubaker (for the state of Alaska) agreed with my proposal, and we set out to test litigate. First, the state passed a statute, drafted by Hawkins, to allow for the bond issuance. Plaintiff Suber was a legal assistant at an Anchorage law firm that represented the plaintiff pro bono. Suber agreed to challenge the validity of the bonds as a taxpayer. Hawkins represented the state's interests.

To litigate the case, I had to research and brief quite a range of constitutional issues, including referendum, public purpose, equal protection, and statutory construction. That work gave me an opportunity to get educated as a bond lawyer—a perfect scholarly storm. The Alaska Supreme Court's opinion in *Suber v. Alaska*[100] reflects almost standard judicial analysis of these issues and found the plan was a public purpose to protect the creditworthiness of the state and was within the "natural disaster" referendum exception.

Shortly after, the state took my advice and formed the Alaska Housing Finance Corporation to finance homeowner mortgages in the state. The bonds included a state enhancement to pay the bonds if repayment of the mortgages did not cover the debt service. Hence, the state assumed responsibility for underwriting and evaluating the creditworthiness of the borrower and, accordingly, the risk of mortgage default.

The Alaska Housing Finance Corporation continues to be the state's primary mortgage lender by issuing both taxable and tax-exempt bonds to attract capital for such mortgages, thereby making it almost unnecessary or impractical, as a business matter, for banks to develop a substantial mortgage lending practice in Alaska. The banks do, however, provide servicing of the mortgages, so they are able to establish commercial relationships with homeowners.

Novel Bonding Purposes

This was to be the first of many financings of novel bonding purposes and which Hawkins determined to test litigate in order to render our approving opinion on behalf of the firm. New York was the state for which Hawkins was the leading public finance firm during my practice years and was the exception. Why? A former judge, Wein, and a citizen, Schultz, each brought numerous lawsuits challenging the validity of various financing statutes, thereby eliminating any need to test litigate. Consequently, New York State has a substantial body of case law that interprets its constitution and under which almost every statute I had drafted upheld the bonds to be issued. That includes those for the New York City Municipal Assistance Corporation (which restructured the city's debt in 1975), the New York Local Government Assistance Corporation (which bonded out the New York State annual spring deficit), the New York City Transitional Authority (which issues bonds for capital purposes secured by the city sales and income tax), and the New York City Water Authority (which completed the third water tunnel with revenue bonds and established meters and rate charges for use of water).

The Connecticut Products Development Corporation and the Indiana Housing Finance Corporation are other entities for which the first bond issue was validated through test litigation, at my request. The Connecticut case validated the issuance of taxpayer-supported bonds to finance venture capital firms and concepts that might, if properly developed, provide new jobs in the state (think of the development of "fuel cells"). The Indiana case validated the issuance of mortgage revenue bonds to finance low- and moderate-income family housing.

Since 1964, public finance law has become more complicated. States and municipalities have been required to expand the purposes for which government provides its taxpayers with infrastructure improvement and services. As the body of legal precedents evolved, test litigation was no longer the first choice of bond counsel. Why? Because either the issue of concern in that state might have already been challenged in another state and a precedent established, or the supposed market standard of "summary judgment" had been diluted by a sense of counsel complacency and market risk acceptance. In other words, a less strict standard seemed to be the norm as the market began accepting a reasoned opinion to the effect that, in a challenge, the validity of the bonds "should be" rather than "must be" upheld.[101] Readers will recall the discussions in Chapters 4 and 5 of the COFINA bond issue in Puerto Rico in which Hawkins rendered its reasoned opinion in 2006.

Public finance law continues to evolve, however. Even where there are clear cases supporting a bond structure, some courts are undertaking review *ab initio*. Recently, for example, the New Jersey Supreme Court reversed many years of precedents upholding bond structures designed to circumvent the constitutional debt limit, but in doing so made the ruling applicable only to future bond authorizations. In Detroit, as noted in an earlier chapter, the bankruptcy court simply excluded from the senior class certain bonds known as certificates of participation. It held that, based on the bankruptcy court's view,[102] the bonds were issued illegally and therefore not entitled to share in the senior class settlement. Those holders accepted ten cents on the dollar rather than litigate that issue, knowing the bias expressed without briefing by the bankruptcy judge.

The lesson to be understood is that under economic pressure of fiscal stress, the validity of bonds is vulnerable. The most noteworthy case is the Washington State Supreme Court case invalidating a then-customary "take or pay contract" for power because the plants financed with that security were no longer needed. The need for power in that area of the county had not expanded, contrary to the feasibility report prepared at the time of the bond issue.[103]

The initial Alaska bond issue spawned several more Alaska public finance experiences. During the time of the initial *Suber* test litigation, unknown to us then, there was an Alaskan resident and taxpayer devoted to no government spending or bonding. As the firm's practice grew in Alaska, this resident repeatedly challenged legislative bond authorizations that were for valid and proper public purposes (e.g., financing a sewer system in the growing borough of Anchorage). His complaints delayed the issuance of the bonds and the availability of the infrastructure. They were repeatedly found by the courts to have no merit. Eventually, his conduct allowed the state to pass a perpetual nuisance statute barring any person who had three or more lawsuits dismissed for being without merit. This was true over any ten-year period from filing a complaint challenging bond authorizations unless he posted a substantial bond that was forfeited if that case was dismissed on first ruling for lack of merit.

After successfully working together on the *Suber* case, Eric Wohlforth and I became the firm's lawyers on the initial Alaska account and several more. In 1966, we hosted a wonderful dinner for Alaska Governor William Egan at the historic Brooklyn restaurant, Gage & Tollner, so we could introduce him to the Wall Street public finance investment bankers.

Our work in Alaska thrived for several years, including expanding to the Greater Anchorage Area Borough. After returning from what had seemed an unnecessary business trip to Alaska, Eric informed me he had decided to move to Alaska. Then he asked if I wanted to join him to practice law there. I declined without giving it much thought.

Princeton College and University of Virginia Law School bred, Eric and his wife of similar cultural background sold their Brooklyn Heights townhouse in 1968 and moved to Anchorage, Alaska, where they raised their children. Eric became the leading bond counsel in the state. However, that was not the end of our personal and professional relationship. Eric (at Wohlforth and Flint), and I (at Hawkins) had many joint retainers as he started out in his financial law practice. Finally, he felt he could render marketable opinions in the name of his own firm, and we switched from co-bond counsel to underwriter's counsel on these financings.

Memorable Trip to Alaska

Over the years, I made many business trips to Alaska, sometimes staying no longer than the day and sometimes flying first class with a work table and champagne to assist my document drafting. One of those trips stands out.

Two investment bankers, an associate from Cravath, Swaine & Moore as underwriter's counsel, and I traveled together from New York to Seattle and then from Seattle to Ketchikan and on to Anchorage. On the first leg from New York to Seattle, I had reserved first class accommodations just for me; I needed time and enough room to draft an indenture for the bond sale. I had to spread out several paper precedents on a bulkhead table to get plenty of room. The flight attendant poured me champagne at regular intervals, resulting in one of my finest pieces of work used as a precedent for other financings.

At Ketchikan, the plane had to turn back from taking off. During its refueling, too much snow had accumulated on the wings for a safe takeoff. As I looked out my window, I saw the special vehicle lift operator was maneuvering under the wing. As I watched, he pushed the button to raise the ladder. To my shock, he had failed to notice he wasn't in front of the wing but directly under it. Consequently, the ladder ascended and broke through the wing, creating a gaping hole.

Ketchikan's airport was actually on an island. We were given the choice of staying in the plane while a boat was sent to the mainland city to obtain the supplies needed to repair the wing (estimated repair time of three hours) or taking that boat into the city and flying out on the next plane a day later. We all chose to stay on the plane, knowing that otherwise the board meeting would have to be delayed, and the bid might have to change to reflect any bond market fluctuation. The airline opened the bar and offered us the drinks we needed for free.

The repair kit retrieved from the mainland consisted of a hair dryer to remove the wing dampness and a wide roll of duct tape. The repair person proceeded to wrap it several times around the wing while another person kept the wing path of the tape heated and dry. Observing the technical quality of the repair, we gulped our drinks and refilled.

While waiting for the repair kit to arrive, the two underwriters discussed the bid that would be submitted for the bonds. They were in agreement about the 5 percent range of interest and were convinced that 5 percent was too low. Accordingly, should we start at 5¾ percent and expect to be negotiated down to 5¼ percent, or start and stand at 5¼? Back and forth it went. They did not seek to exclude me from hearing the debate, knowing I was bond counsel to the issuer and presumably biased. However, in the custom of the industry, bond counsel always had the dual role of representing and being paid by the issuer, while providing the legal opinion to be relied upon by the underwriters and the bond buyers.[104]

Anyway, the two decided to offer the firm 5¼ as the bid and to inform board members it was not open to negotiation. Not wanting to go through that dance, they would make this their first and final bid. That is exactly what happened. The chairman thanked them for such a cost-effective bid. He told everyone at the meeting he knew that, with that rate, the Authority would be able to relend the proceeds to finance home mortgages at rates well under 7 percent. As a result, the proceeds of the bond issuer would be spent quickly, and the Authority would return again to the market.

However, he then said, "Would both of you investment bankers and your counsel please leave and let us discuss our bid in closed-door session?" I was allowed to stay in the private session during which several board members said the bid should be accepted. I then said I had been privy to the discussions on the plane and thought that the bankers were firm. The chairman said he, too, was prepared to take the bid, but he wanted to test the resolve of the bankers and take a stab at a counteroffer. He then opened the door and invited the bankers and counsel back in. He said the board would not accept 5¼ percent; it would accept 5 percent if that would be all right with the bankers. Without a moment's hesitation, the lead banker, Dick Locke, said, "Fine, thank you; we have a deal." He did not even pause to reflect.

I had learned an important lesson. A banker's "first and final" bid is not necessarily his last bid.

On the plane back, I told Locke I would never again stick my neck out to support any bidding by investment bankers. He said his relationship with that board was far more important than a quarter of a point every day, and that if he lost anything on this deal, he would undoubtedly get it back on the next deal.

That night, the board members, underwriters, and all counsel went out for dinner. At the point when everyone was ready to leave, Locke noticed the banker from the other firm had fallen sound asleep, his hand fisted under his chin for support. He took the restaurant check, which was not insubstantial, folded it, and inserted it between two fingers of the sleeping banker. We all proceeded to leave quietly. Outside, the chairman said to me, "That Dick Locke is my kind of guy; sticking the other firm with the check was a perfect retort for falling asleep and ignoring your client."

Whom Can I Trust?

That trip resulted in another lesson for me. On the plane flight to the meeting, the Cravath underwriter's counsel, a senior associate, was drafting the bond purchase agreement (BPA) based on prior precedents I had provided to him. As I was concentrating on the security features of the bond documents, I asked him to confirm he had simply marked up my prior BPA for this deal, making no substantive changes. When he said "yes," I believed him.

When the board accepted the underwriters' bid, it also authorized the bond documents, including the BPA. To my chagrin, upon reviewing the adopted BPA, I found that the Cravath associate had changed a key provision of my firm's disclosure opinion from "nothing has come to our attention regarding certain representations" to "certain representations are true and correct." This change, of course, is more than a legal nicety[105]; it put Hawkins on the hook by vouching for the actual truth of certain facts, a far more difficult legal standard.

On the flight home, I asked him why he had made the change without telling me. I was angry. He casually responded that he figured I'd catch it and revise it. When I reminded him that I said I would not have time to review his draft before the board meeting, he simply shrugged. When I got back to the office, Paul deBary, then a senior associate, and I spent most of the weekend concocting an elaborate recital to document the materials we had reviewed and conversations we had had for "due diligence." Based on the information from those activities only, we rendered the required "true and correct opinion." I was embarrassed and had not wanted to request the consent of the issuer to change back to the traditional negative assurance in a document that the issuer had approved at the meeting. I called the partner-in-charge at Cravath, reiterated the story, and asked that this associate never again be assigned to any of my financings.

That associate was removed from all future deals involving Hawkins, including the Alaska financings.

Lopp's Legacy of Inventiveness

The practice of bond counsel and business solicitation also evolved and, as much as Alaska boosted my career, it also caused me to miss out on one of the largest bond issues in history.

In 1973, I received a call from Jimmy Lopp of Eastman Dillon. Walter James Lopp, "Jimmy," died in 1990 at the age of fifty-one, but he left a legacy of inventiveness in public finance. He is credited with creating the municipal bond insurance business and developing the tax-exempt pollution control bonds at below corporate market interest rates. This would entice major polluters such as paper companies to finance pollution control equipment to clean up the water and air that their facilities had been poisoning for years.[106] He knew I was the bond counsel for the Alaska Industrial Finance Authority and that Alaska was about to authorize the Alyeska pipeline. He told me the federal environmental protection rules required the piping to be covered with a protective liner that would preclude pollution to the air and water environment should the pipe break. Dangers included shifts in the land in which it was embedded, malicious actions of environmentalists, or natural acts such as earthquakes. I told him I would look at the state statute and let him know my view on the applicability of EPA requirements. I would also ask my tax partners to review the federal tax law and determine whether it would qualify for tax-exempt financing. He said if my answer was favorable, he wanted me to accompany him to Juneau to present the concept to my client. Then he asked me to call right back as he wanted to fly up to Alaska the next day.[107]

I called Lopp back six hours later. In the meantime, I had Chuck Kades, our senior tax partner on the tax matter, review the statute that Eric Wohlforth and I had drafted, and I consulted with the managing partner, Don Robinson. Yes, it was a go on both the tax issue and the state statute. Unfortunately, since Hawkins was the bond counsel for the issuer, I could not join him to make the presentation. That would be seen as beyond the scope of the firm's retainer. But I said he could indicate to our client my preliminary approval subject to preparation of a favorable firm memo of law. Bear in mind, the cost of this type of equipment for pollution control purposes would exceed a billion dollars and be the largest tax-exempt financing in history to date.

Lopp was very unhappy with this objection and unaware of any ethical concern. In his view, the bond counsel's role was to render opinions on the validity and tax exemption of the bond for *both* the benefit of the issuer and the benefit of the market. He believed that accompanying a banker with an original financing concept should not be conflict of interest. Today, there is a question whether Dodd-Frank would have allowed even Lopp to make such a presentation. Solicitation of business by an investment banker must be preceded by a presentation to the issuer's financial advisor, thereby compromising the confidentiality of innovative ideas.[108]

My refusal to accompany Lopp prompted him to call his classmate Bob Kutak, a corporate lawyer. Kutak went on that trip *and* the subsequent bond issue became the initial retainer for Kutak and Rock. Today, it's one of the best and biggest firms in the public finance law business.

Roads Not Traveled

Additionally, several nonlegal opportunities came my way. As a result of the *Suber* case and my regular other legal financial service to Alaska as well as meetings with state financial officials, I was recognized by the venerable Drexel Burnham—a leading investment banking firm that appreciated the potential in financing infrastructure in Alaska.

Sometime in 1970, I was invited to lunch with its chairman, who offered me an investment banking position based on his "sources" informing him that the governor respected my ingenuity and contacts in that young state. Because the disparity in pay between public finance bankers and public finance lawyers at that time wasn't significant, I declined. I was enjoying my practice and didn't think I'd be especially effective at pitching public finance products. After all, working with legal precedents and contract covenants were within my comfort zone.

I never regretted rejecting the offer. That firm later spawned junk deal predator Milken and ended up closing.

In the 1990s, I saw the name of my Yale classmate David Clapp inscribed as a major donor of the rebuilt Carnegie Hall. I realized his remuneration as an investment banker in the public finance department of Goldman Sachs and as a firm partner had far exceeded my share of profits as a partner at Hawkins. In 1964, he had confirmed for me that the public finance legal practice and Hawkins suited me well. He went directly from Yale to a small public finance firm specializing in advising universities on their bond issues. After several years of success, he moved to Goldman Sachs where he teamed up with Bob Downey from Dartmouth and two others. They became the most successful public finance investment banking team in history, second to none even today.

At one point early in their association, Gus Levy, then chairman of that venerable firm, was not (in their opinions) properly recognizing their contributions (meaning their bonuses were not comparable to corporate partners). At our invitation, the team "hung out" in our offices for several days awaiting a technical two-week notice period before joining Donaldson Lufkin. Then, as David tells the story in a poor Louisiana-Jewish accent, Gus called him and said, "David, you and your friends come back; we make mistake . . ." The four reneged on Donaldson and returned to Goldman, where, for many more years, they led the investment banking firms in public finance volume and, presumably, profits.

CHAPTER 14

What Are Government-Acquired Development Rights?

From the 1980s on, preserving open space by acquiring the development rights available to farmers and owners of large estates became a popular purpose for using the proceeds of public bond issues. This chapter outlines how one state pioneered a successful approach in the 1970s.

In the mid-1970s, I was asked by the Connecticut state treasurer to make an appointment to see Charlie Stroh, the attorney who represented agricultural interest in the state. Charlie had an office on the third-floor attic of a 1920s craftsman house two streets from the capitol. At the time, the state wanted to resolve how to best preserve the Connecticut farmlands that were producing about 60 percent of fruits and vegetables bought by its residents.

The 1970s was a time of urban sprawl, making farmlands attractive candidates for single-family housing developments and shopping malls. As a result, those families farming the land were being forced to sell because their land was valued high; they couldn't pay the federal and state estate taxes assessed when the patriarch died from their farming profits. Charlie owned a farm himself, but in his case, he raised prized cattle, so the economics of that product provided him immunity from a forced sale.

Charlie and I discussed how a program that bought the "development" rights could achieve the public policy of preserving the farming and parkland if large estates in Connecticut (such as those in Fairfield and Litchfield Counties) were also included. I suggested the cost of acquisition could be paid by a tax on transfer of all land. Why? Because the withdrawal of available land for development such as farm or estate land from the market pool would raise the value of all other land acquisition. He agreed to my approach.

I came back with a draft in which officials from each of Connecticut's 169 towns would determine a selection process for purchasing the development rights of at least one farm or estate in their town. Once a batch of properties was designated, the state bond commission would issue bonds that would be secured by a new 1 percent tax on the existing mortgage recording tax. It would be applied on all property transactions in the state. This self-liquidating fund would preserve the land for farming or open space, and the price paid for the easement would come from the additional mortgage recording tax.

Connecticut Governor Ella T. Grasso rejected outright the increased recording tax proposed. However, she supported the preservation policy by asserting the state would authorize its general obligation bonds to pay for the acquisitions. In other words, Governor Grasso was against increasing the mortgage recording tax to make this a self-liquidating bond program but did support using the general fund taxes to pay the debt service on the bonds.

First in the Nation

While nonprofit entities such as Natural Resources had been using donated funds to buy and place nondevelopment easements on this kind of property, Connecticut's program became the first governmental entity in the nation to buy development rights.[109] Nantucket and Martha's Vineyard in Massachusetts, Suffolk County in New York, and other jurisdictions applied the special tax concept and put perpetual programs in place. In the 1990s, Connecticut passed such an additional recording tax to continue the preservation program.

The issue of "mineral" rights was not raised while drafting this statute. As a result, the developmental rights bought by the state did not address underground rights. Many farmers gained additional revenue by leasing their mineral right to gas companies to build the gas pipeline coming up from Texas. It so happened that Charlie Stroh was the attorney of record for the gas companies in those transactions.

Recent issues arising with these properties for which the development rights were sold to government or acquired as "open space" involve fracking and whether that option to extract gas is restricted or permitted.

Another issue is a commercial use arguably not being a "development." At least one case in Connecticut stopped farm acreage from becoming a golf fairway based on the theory that "development" included any use other than farming. Another case still pending in Suffolk County, NY, concerns a farmhouse becoming a restaurant.

CHAPTER 15

What Is a Chose in Action?

This chapter illustrates that financing and budget options on unique, substantial litigation settlement awards to governments are always available. The most obvious spending option is not necessarily the best or even the most rational.

For years, people were regularly reading about the health hazards of smoking cigarettes, but not until the huge settlement of the litigation by the states with the tobacco companies did health cost and documentation of trends in smoking addiction come to the public's attention.

The Master Settlement Agreement (MSA) between the states and the tobacco companies in 1998 called for annual payments in perpetuity by the tobacco companies to states (and counties in California and New York). The annual amount, which was calculated on cigarette sales in each state, has resulted in billions of dollars being paid.[110]

The initial irony, of course, is that the states had become virtual business partners with the tobacco companies by having a financial stake in sales. The amount of cash anticipated to come in annually became a major policy issue on how to use the bonanza.[111] However, the public preference, shared initially by most politicians, was to use the money for health-related governmental expenses. Since the theory of the settlement amount was premised on the state covering many prior years' healthcare costs, the settlement payments would be appropriated annually to pay ongoing healthcare costs. Several states immediately passed constitutional amendments mandating this money be segregated into a separate fund and used solely for healthcare expenses.

However, public finance investment bankers and others recognized that present-valuing and pledging of future receipts to secure a sizable bond issue was a perfect financing structure to entice public officials to use the annual payments for other than healthcare. That might include major public infrastructure improvements or accumulated deficit payoffs. The legal issues for various bond issuances involved were complicated as well as novel with a need for counsel to opine on antitrust, bankruptcy, and enforcement in detail. This departed from the normal opinion demands of the market. More important, the public policy issues were viewed uniquely because of the substantial amounts involved in settlements.

Securitization of Revenues—Big Business

At the Hawkins firm, I recognized that securitization of these revenues would be big business for many years. So I cajoled those naysayers within Hawkins to focus on making sure we were retained in any role in the first financing in New York.

In the same period, I chaired a National Bond Buyer Conference in San Francisco. Because of my leadership, it became a virtual workshop on how best to structure various offerings. This was particularly true because of the variations based on sales of the cash flow, potential decrease in consumption, need for and reasonableness of retaining an expert on feasibility, and the perpetuity of payments. As a consensus, the industry concluded that, yes, some kind of feasibility report be incorporated into the offering document with calculations on future sales of cigarettes. With that, a new redemption concept was born. The new turbo structure mandated redemption of the amount of bonds equivalent to settlement revenues received in excess of scheduled maturities.

Three Features of Public Policy

I then prepared three features of public policy that caught their attention. They were as follows:

(1) The settlement agreement was based on prior health costs incurred, including treatment for cancer. However, I first suggested it did not follow the path of the revenues awarded as damages going to "healthcare." In fact, the revenues should go to other public purposes or uses that had been "shorted" during those years when the states had appropriated money for healthcare. Certain states such as Mississippi had already passed a constitutional amendment approving the revenue to be put in a healthcare fund. The Mississippi state treasurer readily agreed that his state had not considered my theory properly. But for Mississippi, it was too late.

(2) I also said it was unseemly and unnecessary for the states to be in this long-term partnership with tobacco companies. Taking down the present value of that partnership through a securitization structure could avoid that charge; instead, the bondholders would be taking the revenue risk of sales, especially if the bonds were absolutely non-recourse to the state and issued by a nonentity state-conduit issuer.

(3) I emphasized that securitization was a highly prudent diversification of risk. In fact, most states were already heavily invested in the consumption of sales of cigarettes by reason of the high tax already on cigarette sales.

Those three features of formalizing the fiscal policy spread not only throughout New York and California (which the counties attended) but to almost every state. Hawkins served as bond counsel for many of the transactions, including in the states of Washington, Louisiana, DC, Rhode Island, Iowa, and Ohio, and the counties in New York of Nassau, Westchester, and Erie, as well as several counties in California. The number of deals, the fees generated, the size of the issues, and the new business relationships formed in these various states —plus additional bonds and refunding bonds—went well beyond what even I had anticipated. It fully justified my initial business sense.

Contribution to Business

The most important contribution to the business was twofold: First, Hawkins did the first deal and invested heavily (both partner and associates time) on the cases and disclosure issues affecting the sales of cigarettes. Second, as a leading firm in the securitization structure, Hawkins and three other firms, Orrick, Nixon, and Sidley, became an oligopoly taking on the roles of bond counsel, underwriting counsel, and disclosure counsel.

The other "full service" firms initially had their corporate lawyers in charge rather than their municipal ones. Hawkins became the go-to lawyer firm, particularly because the opinions were so complicated that no other firm could duplicate or pretend expertise without an enormous amount of research. Also, we could price our retainer well by spreading out the cost of that initial effort.

Hawkins also maintained a partner devoted to ongoing due diligence on the technical details of the regular and substantial number of cases that litigated out the kinks in the settlement agreement. The Hawkins' partner knowledgeable about bankruptcy was Roger Bagley. In on the first tobacco securitization deal in the nation, he made a critical contribution to the development of all the deals to come.

Because the basic security was the obligation of private cigarette companies to pay under the Settlement Agreement, the corporate lawyers in those firms initially took control of those deals within their firms. However, it soon became clear the public finance lawyers were needed. Each state (or county) would have to create a special purpose entity to issue tax-exempt bonds secured solely by the settlement payments. The alternative—general obligation bonds—would have unnecessarily implicated the general credit of the issuer in the risk of a shortfall in cigarette sales.

The other firms on this first deal were insisting that, like any new corporate offering of equity for a start-up subsidiary, for tax and corporate law provisions, some sort of equity contribution of 10 percent would be required by the parent company. Hence, these firms were insisting on a current appropriation of that amount by the issuer, Nassau County.

Hawkins, through Bagley, said, "Absolutely not necessary." Nassau County could form a special purpose vehicle and a ring-fenced security structure without any such initial parent (county) contribution, and Hawkins could provide an unqualified straightforward opinion to that effect. The corporate lawyers backed off. I believe the public finance partners in those firms then moved in to claim these tobacco securitizations as the domain of the public finance departments.

At Hawkins, our whole firm was public finance, so we had none of that interoffice conflict about which department would be in charge of the deals. We had issues of partners claiming credit for the new clients retaining us for these unique transactions. However, that didn't include the corporate versus public finance power struggle prevalent in the investment banking firms, the banks, and the bigger law firms.

While busy working on the various county securitizations in New York, I patiently waited for my California partners to start working on these deals in California. The Orrick firm, which was the leading public finance firm in California, was counseling the investment bankers and the state and counties that authorizing state legislation came before any securitization could go forward. My West Coast partners ignored my urging to do their own research, so I started my own review of the California constitution and the statutes respecting financing by state and local governments. I had done deals in California long before we had offices there, so I was not a novice to the provisions of the California constitution.

A Chose in Action

I learned that the simple answer of law was right there for everybody to read. The state government and each county had explicit statutory power to sell real and personal property. I then researched what was the legal category of a Master Settlement Agreement. Based on several opinions of the highest court in California, a judgment for damages —a settlement arising out of contested litigation—was legally called "a chose in action" or "a thing." That "thing" was considered a personal property right—one that could be hypothecated and sold because it didn't go against any public policy to do so. In fact, litigants with such awards or judgments would either sell their rights to future money or use it as collateral for loans. No big legal deal—the county and state had straightforward statutory power to sell "personal property."

My former associate and partner in California, Kevin Civale, and I went off to visit investment bankers and officials in every county and in the state itself. We announced we would render the tobacco securitization opinions and do the deals without qualification and, most important, without any new legislation. Once we embarrassed them with their failure to read the law the way I did, even Orrick followed. It was a clear and logical analysis that was never challenged. Hawkins was retained in almost every financing done in California, including by the state government itself.

Interestingly, the policy decision made by California and New York was to devise a structure that backed the bonds with the state moral obligation credit. It would enhance the security structure, achieve higher ratings, reduce the debt service payment risk, and therefore be entitled to receive substantially more up-front cash with the interest rate being reduced to produce greater present value. In other words, the two states backed the payments to be made by the tobacco companies in return for a larger amount of proceeds from the securitization.

An unfortunate result for those states that didn't choose to "securitize" their future payments is the decline in cigarette sales. That means the actual amount being received is nowhere as much as expected. However, the states that did choose to do those deals received present value on an optimistic feasibility report on those future sales.

Payments of debt service on bonds sold based on those feasibility studies were not materially adversely affected. Why? Because they were sold usually with two times the coverage, and the sales decline has not yet been that steep. Furthermore, most initial bonds sold in the *previous* century have been refunded at reduced interest rates in *this* century. As a result, additional present value benefits have been received.

Since the annual payments from the tobacco companies are to be made in perpetuity, regular securitization deals are continuing but are not as "rich" because of a decline in anticipated revenues from the declining estimated sales curve of cigarettes.

Richard Land Sigal practiced public finance from 1964 to 2016, including fifty years with the national law firm of Hawkins Delafield & Wood. He was the bond counsel or underwriters' partner in charge of major tax exempt or taxable bond issues in many states as well as the Commonwealth of Puerto Rico. A graduate of Yale University (1960) and the University of Chicago School of Law (1963), Sigal's contribution to the creation of financing strategies to support the growth of public infrastructure are unmatched.

- During his career, Sigal crafted innovative, precedent-setting public finance structures, including:

- First Clean Water Bond program that leveraged federal water and sewer grants

- First revenue bonds secured by state income or sales tax that restructured New York City debt in 1975, funded the multi-billion-dollar New York State Spring borrowing in 1983, and first securitization of those revenues to finance each of New York City's and New York State's new capital programs

- First bond securitization of the annual in-perpetuity payments of the major tobacco companies to states and the counties in New York and California to fund major infrastructure programs

- First public-private partnerships to finance waste-to-energy plants based on put-or-pay delivery contracts of municipalities to private corporations with patented technology

- First state "first-time homebuyer" and low- and moderate-housing finance general bond resolution (not project-by-project financings)

- First state venture capital finance program

- First statewide program to acquire development rights of farmland

- First multiyear, multibillion-dollar program to modernize a state's flagship university

- First tax-exempt bond programs to finance new sources of power or to stabilize existing power authorities secured by statutorily mandated utility charges

Among his most significant contributions was developing a special tax in 2006 to secure a multibillion-dollar bond issue to fund general fund deficits of the Commonwealth of Puerto Rico. That security structure withstood a challenge in 2019 during the recent Puerto Rico bankruptcy. It is expected to be used as a prime structure to finance the many new capital needs of that territory.

Mr. Sigal was a two-year chairman of the New York State Bar Association—Municipal Law Section, chairman of Bond Buyer National Conferences held in San Francisco and New York and received the Corporate Affiliate Award in 2008 for outstanding service to the profession and the National Association of State Treasurers.

Mr. Sigal resides in New York City with his wife Samayla Deutch, who is also an attorney.

Visit his web site at: RichardLandSigal.com

ACKNOWLEDGMENTS

I'm grateful for the assistance of Deirdre Roney, Esq. in tracking down references and clarifying my sentences. I also appreciate the encouragement and assistance from Laurie Schwartz, Esq. Both lawyers are former associates who contributed to the bond issue case studies described in this book. I am also grateful for the Dudley Court Press team, who made both volumes of this work come to life.

From: "Richard L. Sigal" <richardlsigal@gmail.com>
Date: July 25, 2013 at 6:30:07 PM EDT
To: Andy Dillon <DillonA2@michigan.gov>
Subject: Detroit

I am responding to your last email about Detroit being different and just cannot handle the taxes to cover the debt and other liabilities. I may at some point agree with that but not yet and here is why and my respect for "process."

Detroit has issued full faith and credit debt which is the municipal nomenclature for "good faith dealings" embedded as a legal term in all business contracts. My "new approach" memo ended with a restructured debt settlement whereas it should have been prefaced by what I had in mind as a first step; the preparation of an inventory of the assets of the city, the values of those assets and availability of monetizing those to reduce the debt and other liabilities. What seems to be missing in Detroit is that the 10 cents on the dollar was the first demand by the bankruptcy lawyers and the lines immediately hardened.

Naturally, litigation was the result and now a lengthy controversial period will ensue rather than there good faith negotiations before the bankruptcy filing. This works well for the bankruptcy lawyers who can run up their bill litigating rather than spending legal dollars working for a consensus.

"Is the city really insolvent?" is a basic question as a business matter. Forget the technical bankruptcy definition which is absurd for municipal bankruptcy. One of the richest counties in America, Orange County, qualified under Chapter 9 because it did not have the money in the bank to meet the claims of the pooled participants while it had ready access to the bond market to raise the cash.

Suggest to the bankruptcy court to order a standstill agreement now among all litigants and have the governor activate an advisory board (with Felix Rohatyn and City leaders and with me as counsel to it) to immediately engage in good faith negotiations without demands with all stakeholders and that the board seek ways and means to monetize the city assets while mindful that the city must spend immediate dollars for police, fire, sanitation, and street lighting. Each member of the board and we review a inventory plan that anticipates looking at those assets such as the art collection, the development of distressed city land, parking garages, and bridge tolls as well the resources of the county, proposals to provide various services by private nonprofit or equity players, etc.

Give us three weeks to prepare the outreach plan and then allocate board members with the relationships to actually reach out.

Give us three months to do that and if there is no meaningful progress that we "good guys" can be successful then back to the Orr / Jones "cramdown" approach.

If you do that, then you have honored and exercised the good faith contract pledge in the City bonds and you can go forward with the cramdown demands that the bankruptcy lawyers are advocating and litigating.

In other words, you have RIGHT now that good faith window rather than spending the litigation dollars contesting whether you did or did not exercise good faith prior to this with the Orr/Jones team. And you will have the clear "evidence" of fairness required for a plan approval with this approach.

Consider letting me try this New York approach with that Advisory Board in this immediate period in lieu of litigating for that period. Then if we cannot get the "assets" as resources at sufficient levels to reduce significantly the liabilities the state can then fully proceed with the cramdown having fully satisfied the good faith dealings of the bond contracts and the condition precedent of the bankruptcy filing.

Andy, I am ready any time to come out to discuss but time is of the essence as positions start to harden and unfortunately the Detroit taxpayers have been sidelined with no advocate as the Governor has forced this on the Mayor and his lawyers, not city lawyers that are taking charge.

Letter to Bankruptcy Counsel

Congratulations on such a success for the Seniors. I am particularly pleased the COFINA structure held together despite the challenges. Bond counsel and bankruptcy counsel have different roles. You fought and won by a walk-off grand slam in baseball terms for your client the seniors and deserve all including the success fee.

But in my view Puerto Rico is totally shut out and will stay shut out of the capital markets for years. Why?

First: PROMESA returned it to a territory under federal control and how does one stop by contract law a second PROMESA in the future so what contract protection and assurance do the underwriters of a new-money bond issue have?

Second: Not taking the step of actually fully litigating the clawback challenge by the go holders leaves any COFINA new bond issue or even an income tax securitization similarly structured with the same risk of clawback challenge.

I understand you did your best to exclude your clients' bonds taken in exchange by getting the court sign off so a Fifth Amendment takings probably protects those bonds from either of the issues referenced above for new money.

Therefore Puerto Rico, despite so much time money and whatever, will not emerge with a marketable bond structure for its capital needs and undoubtedly will need federal enhancement or guarantees.

My basic job in all my workout retainers such as MAC in NYC, Yonkers, Bridgeport, Waterbury and Orange County was to restructure and remarket debt so the issuer could recover and continue with market access.

Walking Down Wall Street Circa 1964

In 1964, starting at the top of Broadway at Trinity Church, Wall Street was home to the headquarters or major offices of the Bank of New York (founded by Alexander Hamilton), Bank of Manhattan (founded by Aaron Burr), Irving Trust, Bankers Trust, Manufacturers Hanover Trust, New York Stock Exchange, J. P. Morgan Bank, Seamans Savings Bank, U.S. Trust, Dillon Read, Brown Brothers Harriman, and the venerable AIG (American International Group, Inc.), the behemoth insurance company. The old-line law firms were Carter Ledyard & Milburn; Milbank, Tweed, Hadley & McCloy; Sullivan & Cromwell; and Shearman & Sterling, counsel to First National City Bank and headquartered above its landmarked building. They were also located on Wall Street, along with the venerable Salomon Brothers and First Boston, which was located nearby at Exchange Place. The area featured several private or exclusive lunch clubs, including the India House, Wall Street Club, Downtown Association, Lunch Club, Bankers Club, and Harry's steak/lobster restaurant. Each was discretely lodged in its own spacious townhouses or lavishly spread across a full floor of an office building. Harry's, located in the basement of the India House, was the exception.

Harry was the steak house's legendary proprietor, featured several times in the *Wall Street Journal*. He was known for remembering everyone's name, hosting a popular Friday night "watering hole" for bond dealers, and extending credit whenever the vicissitudes of working on Wall Street left one without a paycheck for a time.

The 1960s office building credited with anchoring the Wall Street financial district for the rest of the twentieth century was the Chase Manhattan Plaza built by David Rockefeller. It was not on Wall Street, though, but a block away from it.

The late twentieth-century merger mania of these major money banks is fascinating in itself, epitomized as follows: the Bank of Manhattan merged in 1955 with Chase National Bank and was acquired by Chemical Bank in 1996 (retaining the Chase name). In 2000, Chase acquired J. P. Morgan & Co. (making it JPMorgan Chase), and in 2008 it acquired Bear Stearns.

Today, Wall Street has been all but abandoned by "Wall Street" financial firms. Instead, it has been restructured for housing and high-end retail shops after the downtown shifted to the World Trade Center in Battery Park City. AIG remains at 110 Wall Street while Bankers Trust merged with Alex Brown & Sons and was acquired by Deutsche Bank. Deutsche Bank later bought and moved into the J. P. Morgan headquarters building built in 1989 at 60 Wall Street. Trump International at 40 Wall—the original Bank of Manhattan Company Building—remains the only general purpose office building on Wall Street.

Of course, the venerable New York Stock Exchange remains at the intersection of Broad Street and Wall Street. There, specialists continue to trade by hand signals walking around on the floor during their eight regular office hours. However, many more shares are traded by computer transactions while several investment banks have their own floor-wide computer trading operations with white-shirted traders sitting in front of Bloomberg terminals.

Preface and Introduction

[1] Robert Mcg. Thomas Jr., "Charles Kades, 90, Architect of Japan's Postwar Charter," *N.Y. Times,* June 21, 1996, *https://www.nytimes.com/1996/06/21/world/charles-kades-90-architect-of-japan-s-postwar-charter.html*

[2] Bankruptcy is part of the U.S. Constitution, Article 1, Section 8, and is codified in Title 11 of the U.S. Code. See Wasson and Thornhill, "Bankruptcy in the U.S. Constitution and Laws," April 4, 2016. *https://wassonthornhill.com/bankruptcy-u-s-constitution-laws/.* For a basic outline on bankruptcy law, see: U.S. Courts, "Chapter 9 – Bankruptcy Basics" at *https://www.uscourts.gov/services-forms/bankruptcy/bankruptcy-basics/chapter-9-bankruptcy-basics.*

[3] See Hillary Russ, "Bankruptcy saves tiny Rhode Island city, but leaves scars," Reuters, September 3, 2012, *https://www.reuters.com/article/us-usa-rhodeisland-centralfalls-bankrupt-idUSBRE88300220120904* .

[4] "The U.S. Senate passed the bill known by its acronym PROMESA . . . three weeks after the House overwhelmingly backed the measure." Stephen Nuno-Perez, "Congress Passes PROMESA Act for Puerto Rico Debt Crisis," NBC News, June 29, 2016, *https://www.nbcnews.com/news/latino/congress-passes-promesa-act-puerto-rico-debt-crisis-n601291.*

[5] "Investing in infrastructure is foundational to these efforts. Not only does infrastructure serve as a platform to support industries and broader regional growth, but it can also be a driver of more equitable and enduring growth for individuals. After all, constructing and maintaining reliable roads, ports, pipes, and other systems is essential to all types of businesses and households. Whether moving passengers and goods or ensuring that water, electricity, and broadband is available to everyone, both the public and private sector have a shared responsibility to oversee these various systems. Yet even beyond this supportive role, many local leaders overlook another significant opportunity: Infrastructure can also represent a key economic anchor." Joseph Kane, "Recognizing Infrastructure's Role as a Local Economic Anchor," Brookings Institute, August 10, 2018, *https://www.brookings.edu/blog/the-avenue/2018/08/10/recognizing-infrastructures-role-as-a-local-economic-anchor.*

[6] Trump: "To help build a better future for all Americans, I ask the Congress to act soon on an infrastructure bill that will: stimulate at least $1.5 trillion in new investment over the next 10 years, shorten the process for approving projects to 2 years or less, address unmet rural infrastructure needs, empower State and local authorities, and train the American workforce of the future … My Administration's plan addresses more than traditional infrastructure—like roads, bridges, and airports—but addresses other needs like drinking and wastewater systems, waterways, water resources, energy, rural infrastructure, public lands, veterans' hospitals, and Brownfield and Superfund sites. The reforms set forth in my plan will strengthen the economy, make our country more competitive, reduce the costs of goods and services for American families, and enable Americans to build their lives on top of the best infrastructure in the world." Legislative Outline for Rebuilding Infrastructure in America, Feb. 12, 2018, transmission letter, *https://www.whitehouse.gov/wp-content/uploads/2018/02/INFRASTRUCTURE-211.pdf.*

[7] In May 2019, a bipartisan group of elected Congress persons published an excellent blueprint plan for comprehensive infrastructure in the United States featuring financial solutions including state and local bond financing. *https://reed.house.gov/uploadedfiles/2019_problem_solvers_caucus_infrastructure_report.pdf.*

[8] "Unless pension funds around the nation continue to earn 7% or more per year on their investments, it's likely that taxpayers will be on the hook for trillions of dollars of promises to government unions." Chuck DeVore, "$5.2 Trillion Of Government Pension Debt Threatens To Overwhelm State Budgets, Taxpayers," *Forbes*, May 31, 2019, *https://www.forbes.com/sites/chuckdevore/2019/05/31/5-2-trillion-of-government-pension-debt-threatens-to-overwhelm-state-budgets-taxpayers/.*

[9] "Nuveen, a perennial bull on risky municipal debt, is planning a new fund to invest in state and local government bonds in distress, default or in bankruptcy, according to a securities filing." Martin Z Braun, "Muni-Junk Titan Nuveen Starts Fund to Take Advantage of Defaults," Bloomberg, May 24, 2019, *https://www.bloomberg.com/news/articles/2019-05-24/major-muni-junk-bond-buyer-starts-fund-to-capitalize-on-defaults.*

Chapters

[1] Hawkins Delafield & Wood LLP was founded in 1854 and has ninety lawyers in nine offices across the U.S.

[2] Clean water bonds are issued to fund "water quality improvement projects in the United States." Wikipedia, "Clean Water State Revolving Fund," *https://en.wikipedia.org/wiki/Clean_Water_State_Revolving_Fund.*

[3] "Mortgage revenue bonds (MRBs) are bonds issued by local or state Housing Finance Agencies (HFAs). The HFA will issue the tax-free bonds to investors. Funding from the sale of these bonds is then used to finance affordable mortgages for low- and middle-income people." Reviewed by James Chen, "Mortgage Revenue Bond (MRB)," Investopedia, May 8, 2018, *https://www.investopedia.com/terms/m/mortgage-revenue-bond.asp.*

[4] A pollution control bond is a "municipal revenue bond in which debt service is secured by payments from a private firm using pollution control equipment that the bond was used to finance. Thus, the guarantee of repayment is made by the private firm rather than by the municipal issuer. For pollution control bonds issued before August 8, 1986, interest is free from federal taxation. Tax reform passed in 1986 eliminated this exemption. Interest on pollution control bonds issued on or after August 8, 1986, is fully taxable." David L. Scott, "Pollution Control Bond" in *The Free Dictionary* by *Wall Street Words: An A to Z Guide to Investment Terms for Today's Investor,* *https://financial-dictionary.thefreedictionary.com/pollution+control+bond.*

[5] "In finance, a tobacco bond is a type of US bond issued by a state to obtain immediate cash backed up with a won lawsuit against a tobacco company." Wikipedia, "Tobacco Bond," *https://en.wikipedia.org/wiki/Tobacco_bond.*

[6] Robert Caro, *The Power Broker: Robert Moses and the Fall of New York* (New York: Vintage, 1975).

[7] "The New York Constitution appears to place severe restrictions on the power of the state and its local governmental units to incur financial liabilities … Forty-four states have enacted constitutional limitations on borrowing power similar to some or all of New York's provisions; two require greater-than majority votes of the legislature, and all others require either a referendum or a constitutional amendment before the state can contract most forms of indebtedness." Michael D. Utevsky, "The Future of Nonguaranteed Bond Financing in New York," *Fordham Law Review* 45, no. 4, Art. 12 (1977): 863–64, *https://ir.lawnet.fordham.edu/flr/vol45/iss4/12/.*

[8] The city had outstanding notes in the billions maturing in 1975 for which it was expected the notes would be remarketed for another year. The city had anticipated federal revenue sharing to repay those notes, but that program was terminated. Hence, there was a need to bond out the notes. Michael D. Utevsky, "The Future of Nonguaranteed Bond Financing in New York," *Fordham Law Review* 45, no. 4, Art. 12 (1977): 863–64, *https://ir.lawnet. fordham.edu/flr/vol45/iss4/12/*.

[9] For the technical, legal history of the cases in New York on this matter, see Gayle Gutekunst-Roth, "Note: New York – A City in Crisis: Fiscal Emergency Legislation and the Constitutional Attacks," *Fordham Urban Law Journal* 6, no. 1, Art. 3, (1977).

[10] "Gov. Hugh L. Carey, among others, argues that Mr. Ford's public recalcitrance bought time for the city to make its case to an even more reluctant Congress … Moreover, the speech spurred New York's civic, business and labor leaders to rally bankers in the United States and abroad, who feared their own investments would be harmed if New York defaulted on its debt … With 30 years' hindsight, some of the players say that if Mr. Ford had acquiesced to the city's appeals months or even weeks earlier, New York might never have recovered. Ford was good for New York, because he made us clean up our act." Sam Roberts, "Infamous 'Drop Dead' Was Never Said by Ford," *N.Y. Times*, December 28, 2006, *https://www.nytimes.com/2006/12/28/ nyregion/28veto.html*. E.J. McMahon, "The Man Who Saved New York," *New York Post*, July 25, 2010, *https://nypost.com/2010/07/25/the-man-who-saved-new-york*.

[11] "Like a thunderclap, the State Court of Appeals decision invalidating the moratorium on the payment of $1 billion in short-term New York City notes sent all the participants in the city's long running fiscal drama scrambling for cover in different directions in the last week … Many lawyers who read the decision's assertion that noteholders were 'not entitled' to payment until it could he arranged not to be 'unnecessarily disruptive' of the city's finances said that the effect of the Court of Appeals action was to bring about a sort of judicial moratorium in place of the legislative moratorium it had so roundly denounced." Steven R. Weisman, "Invalidation of Moratorium on New York City Notes Is Called Dawn of New Reality," *N.Y. Times*, November 25, 1976, *https://www.nytimes.com/1976/11/25/archives/invalidation-of-moratorium-new-york-city-notes-is-called-dawn-of.html*. The *New York Times* article is discussing *Flushing Nat. Bank v. MAC*, 40 N.Y.2d 731, 1976, available at *https://law. justia.com/cases/new-york/court-of-appeals/1976/40-n-y-2d-731-0.html*.

¹² "Still licking its wounds from the past, this aging metropolis continues to suffer from a bruised public image—earned in part from years of rancor over a federally mandated integration order, decades of failure to control its municipal finances, and a long line of ill-fated mayors (not to mention its reputation for political corruption). Yonkers, as the saying goes, is 'the city of hills where nothing is on the level.'" Elsa Brenner, "A Tarnished Yonkers Survives but Finds That It Still Suffers," *N.Y. Times*, October 5, 1997, *http://www.nytimes.com/1997/10/05/nyregion/a-tarnished-yonkers-survives-but-finds-that-it-still-suffers.html.*

¹³ "But State Comptroller Edward V. Regan said today that he could not certify the Yonkers budget until the money was appropriated by the Legislature, or unless Yonkers made cuts to bring its budget into balance without the state aid . . . Yonkers had hoped for $10.5 million, and Eugene J. Fox, the Yonkers City Manager, called the Albany agreement 'very disappointing. The consequences on our proposed budget will be far-reaching and serious,' he said. 'Albany doesn't know what it's doing.'" E. J. Dionne Jr., "State Aid to Cities Resolved; Yonkers Upset by Allotment," *N.Y. Times*, July 24, 1981, *http://www.nytimes.com/1981/07/24/nyregion/state-aid-to-cities-resolved-yonkers-upset-by-allotment.html.* Josh Barbanel, "Regan Relates Roles in Certifying Budget for Yonkers in 1983," *N.Y. Times*, April 19, 1984, *http://www.nytimes.com/1984/04/19/nyregion/regan-relates-role-in-certifying-budget-for-yonkers-in-1983.html.*

¹⁴ "The legislation that I will be signing into law will make the program an even greater success. It will extend revenue sharing from another 3 ¾ years. It will provide $25,600 million to State and local units of government." "Gerald R. Ford: Remarks in Yonkers, New York, Upon Signing the State and Local Fiscal Assistance Amendments of 1976," available at *http://www.presidency.ucsb.edu/ws/?pid=6454.*

¹⁵ "Judge Leonard B. Sand of United States District Court in Manhattan signed off on the settlement agreement that officials in Yonkers and the local N.A.A.C.P. president, Karen Edmonson, approved two weeks ago. In announcing his decision, Judge Sand formally put an end to 27 years of often hostile litigation—a battle that turned out to be so costly it almost drove Yonkers into bankruptcy." Fernanda Santos, "After 27 Years, Yonkers Housing Desegregation Battle Ends Quietly in Manhattan Court," *N.Y. Times*, May 2, 2007, *https://www.nytimes.com/2007/05/02/nyregion/02yonkers.html.*

¹⁶ "Ordered that the fines imposed by this Court's August 2, 1988 finding of contempt against the City of Yonkers, and the collection and payment

thereof, shall not supersede, pre-empt, or otherwise in any way be accorded priority over pre-existing liens and obligations to bondholders." *U.S.A. and Yonkers Branch-NAACP v. Yonkers Bd. of Educ.*, et al., 80 Civ. 6761 Order, S.D.N.Y. (Sept. 2, 1998).

[17] Merton H. Miller and David J. Ross, "The Orange County Bankruptcy and its Aftermath: Some New Evidence," *Journal of Derivatives* 4, no. 4 (Summer 1997): 51–60.

[18] The Orange County fiasco case led to multiple charges and settlements. C.S. First Boston Corp. settled federal charges and paid fines. SEC settled charges against Orange County and several of its officials, and a criminal investigation against Merrill Lynch & Co. Robert L. Citron and Matthew R. Raabe faced criminal charges. E. Scott Rechard, "O.C. Bankruptcy Case Settled by First Boston," *L.A. Times*, January 30, 1998, *http://articles.latimes.com/1998/jan/30/news/mn-13691*.

[19] The surrounding municipalities had readily invested their pensions, because the rate of returns was spectacular for some time. However, the fund manager or his lawyers did not think to restrict withdrawal of the investments only for payment of the pensions. If such a restriction were in place, the panic for the paper loss and withdrawal could have been prevented.

[20] "Orange County, one of the richest in the United States, has incurred substantial losses through mismanagement by one of its officials . . . The county profited immensely for many years by gambling on the market, and should not face its losses. Orange County, and the state of California, has ample resources to see that no municipal bondholder loses any money, and that all creditors are paid." Philip M. Dearborn, "The Municipal Bankruptcy Dodge," *The Washington Post*, December 22, 1994.

[21] "Lawyers on Monday asked a federal judge to approve a $48-million bonus they say Orange County owes them for handling the county's complex bankruptcy litigation. The request, filed by the law firm of Hennigan, Mercer & Bennett, is in addition to the $26 million in hourly fees the firm has already collected. If approved by U.S. District Judge Gary L. Taylor, it would boost the firm's total compensation to 8.5 percent of the $865 million it won in settlements with Merrill Lynch & Co. and other companies accused of helping cause the county's 1994 financial collapse." David Reyes, "O.C. Bankruptcy Lawyers Ask Judge to OK $48-Million Bonus," *LA Times*, August 24, 1999, *http://articles.latimes.com/keyword/thomas-w-hayes*.

²² Merton H. Miller and David J. Ross, "The Orange County Bankruptcy and its Aftermath: Some New Evidence," *Journal of Derivatives* 4, no. 4 (Summer 1997): 51–60. E. Scott Rechard, "O.C. Bankruptcy Case Settled by First Boston," *LA Times*, January 30, 1998, *http://articles.latimes.com/1998/jan/30/news/mn-13691*.

²³ One book written in 1998 does a decent report about the Orange County bankruptcy. It notes that neighboring San Diego County prevented withdrawals by its pool participants by penalizing or offering the option of waiting "until financial markets cooled down. San Diego pool participants chose to wait." The book suggests that bankruptcy should not be the first choice as happened in 0range County and that building consensus with the affected participants is always the best way. But even this book focuses more on the mark-to-market aspect of the pool analysis than on the proper scheduling of the invested securities' maturities to have the cash ready to pay out for pensions obligations. Mark Baldassare, *When Government Fails, the Orange County Bankruptcy* (Oakland, CA: University of California Press, a joint publication with the Public Policy Institute of California, 1998).

²⁴ Merton H. Miller and David J. Ross, "The Orange County Bankruptcy and its Aftermath: Some New Evidence," *Journal of Derivatives* 4, no. 4 (Summer 1997): 51–60. E. Scott Rechard, "O.C. Bankruptcy Case Settled by First Boston," *LA Times*, January 30, 1998, *http://articles.latimes.com/1998/jan/30/news/mn-13691*.

²⁵ Michael M. Rosen, "Obama vs. the 'Speculators,'" Politico, May 30, 2009, *https://www.politico.com/story/2009/05/obama-vs-the-speculators-022424*.

²⁶ A summary outline of the city's financial woes starting in 2005. Associated Press, "Timeline of Detroit's Financial Crisis," *Washington Times*, November 7, 2017, *https://www.washingtontimes.com/news/2014/nov/7/timeline-of-detroits-financial-crisis/*.

²⁷ "Of greatest value is the city's art collection. Yes, Detroit actually has a world class art collection. Its museum is over a hundred years old, is the second largest municipally-owned museum in the country, owns some 65,000 works, and is considered to have one of the top six collections in the U.S. It has special emphasis on American artists, with what is considered to be the second best American collection in the country. The city also owns real estate beneath the collection. The collection's value is being assessed by Christie's, and most experts agree that the value is somewhere around a billion dollars. It would be a bummer to have to sell off the entire thing, although doing so would

raise enough money to cover both the $326 million deficit and the $600 million in unfunded pensions, while leaving some money left over to carry the city into next year. And while nobody wants to see the museum close, the collection would find its way into deserving hands that would take care of it. It's not like these are stray puppies that won't find a home and end up in a kill shelter. On the other hand, selling the collection isn't even necessary. Money is lent against art all the time by specialty finance firms. A 50–60% LTV, probably an 8–10% annualized interest rate, would go a long way towards solving near-term cash issues." Lawrence Meyers, "Muni Bonds: A Case Study of Detroit's Fiasco," LearnBonds.com, October 25, 2013, *https://learnbonds.com/news/detroit-bankruptcy-municipal-bonds/.*

[28] As discussed in the preceding endnote, the value of the collection was sufficient to cover the city's obligations.

[29] Let me provide my credentials to discuss the mess in Puerto Rico. While we had been retained by the Commonwealth's Government Development Bank on housing finance issue in the 1990s, in 2005 we were retained to develop a financing structure to bond out what was in effect general fund deficits. We researched well and based on the New York State case law and similarities between New York and Puerto Rico's constitutions determined a sales tax securitization structure ("COFINA") would be sustained if challenged. The underwriters were able to market the $3 billion of bonds with that reasoned opinion. Another firm replaced us for a third, and more, issues and developed a subordinated issue providing a similar reasoned approving opinion.

[30] *Sovereign Debt Management* by Rosa Lastra and Lee Buchhei (Oxford University Press, 2014) lays out a path to lessen a country's national debt by, in essence, short-changing its creditors. The explicit details of the process outlined in the book was essentially replicated during the period Cleary was representing Puerto Rico.

[31] "Puerto Rico's governor, saying he needs to pull the island out of a 'death spiral,' has concluded that the Commonwealth cannot pay its roughly $72 billion in debts, an admission that will probably have wide-reaching financial repercussions." Michael Corkery and Mary Williams Walsh, "Puerto Rico's Governor Says Island's Debts Are 'Not Payable,'" *N.Y. Times,* June 28, 2015, *https://www.nytimes.com/2015/06/29/business/dealbook/puerto-ricos-governor-says-islands-debts-are-not-payable.html.*

[32] "Senators Elizabeth Warren (D-Massachusetts) and Bernie Sanders (I-Vermont) introduced on Wednesday a bill that would effectively erase billions of dollars in debt owed by Puerto Rico and other American territories ravaged by hurricanes (and Wall Street) in recent years." Jack Herrera, "Could a New Bill Free Puerto Rico From Its Debt?" *Pacific Standard Magazine*, July 25, 2018, *https://psmag.com/news/warren-and-sanders-introduce-bill-to-end-puerto-rico-debt.*

[33] "Assured Guaranty Municipal Corp. (AGM), a bond insurance subsidiary of Bermuda-based holding company Assured Guaranty Ltd, has agreed to terms of the agreement in principle resolving how Puerto Rico sales-and-use-tax (IVU by its Spanish acronym) revenues will be divided between holders of senior and subordinate bonds issued by the Puerto Rico Sales Tax Financing Corp. (COFINA by its Spanish acronym) and secured by IVU revenues. The most recent agreement is supported by senior and subordinate COFINA creditors, including AGM–representing about $10 billion of the public corporation's debt—as well as the island's Financial Oversight and Management Board and government." Eva Llorens Velez, "Assured Guaranty joins agreement between senior, subordinate COFINA bondholders," *Caribbean Business*, August 9, 2018, *http://caribbeanbusiness.com/assured-guaranty-joins-agreement-between-senior-subordinate-cofina-bondholders.*

[34] "Puerto Rico's Financial Oversight and Management Board and governor both announced that the board—as representative of the Puerto Rico Sales Tax Financing Corp. (COFINA by its Spanish acronym) in the bankruptcy-like process under Title III of the Puerto Rico Oversight, Management, and Economic Stability Act (Promesa)—the government and a number of bondholders reached a deal to restructure the instrumentality's debt. The 'agreement in principle' reached with senior and junior bondholders and monoline insurers includes new COFINA securities under 'terms that are aligned with the fiscal reality of Puerto Rico,' according to the release issued by the office of Gov. Ricardo Rosselló. The deal provides for more than a 32 percent reduction in COFINA debt, providing Puerto Rico about $17.5 billion in future debt-service payments and provides terms and conditions for restructuring the government-owned corporation's debt." *Caribbean Business*, "Puerto Rico fiscal board, gov: Deal with COFINA bondholders reached," August 8, 2018, *http://caribbeanbusiness.com/puerto-rico-fiscal-board-gov-deal-with-cofina-bondholders-reached.*

[35] Court date to review Puerto Rico's debt restructuring deal. Eva Llorens Velez, "Court could hear Puerto Rico GDB's debt-restructuring deal in November," *Caribbean Business*, August 1, 2018, *http://caribbeanbusiness.com/court-could-hear-puerto-rico-gdbs-debt-restructuring-deal-in-november.*

[36] "Under the new RSA, bondholders can exchange their outstanding bonds for two classes of new securitization bonds: Tranche A bonds will be exchanged at 67.5 cents on the dollar and are expected to mature in 40 years; Tranche B 'growth' bonds 'will be tied to the economic recovery of Puerto Rico' and mature in 45 years. The latter will be exchanged at 10 cents on the dollar, both the board and the administration said." *Caribbean Business*, "Preliminary agreement with Puerto Rico power utility bondholders reached," July 30, 2018, *http://caribbeanbusiness.com/preliminary-agreement-with-puerto-rico-power-utility-creditors-reached.*

[37] Judge Swain approved over $19 million in legal fees, but millions more worth of fees are still under review. Eva Llorens Velez, "Swain's World: Legal Workers Rolling in Bankruptcy Dough," *Caribbean Business*, July 27, 2018, *http://caribbeanbusiness.com/swains-world-legal-workers-rolling-in-bankruptcy-dough/.*

[38] Jonathan Oosting, "Michigan Treasurer Andy Dillon resigns, citing messy divorce and media scrutiny," MLive, October 11, 2013, *https://www.mlive.com/politics/2013/10/andy_dillon_resigns_michigan_t.html;* MFI Miami, "Is Andy Dillon Dragging Michigan Down with Him in His Losing Battle with Booze?" August 2013, *https://mfi-miami.com/2013/08/andy-dillon/.*

[39] According to *Black's Law Dictionary*, adhesion contracts are contracts offered on an essentially "take it or leave it" basis. The legal trend is to relieve the contract party from the onerous conditions.

[40] "E-mails between Gov. Rick Snyder's administration, Kevyn Orr and Jones Day law firm reveal the governor's early plan to take Detroit into bankruptcy before City Council approved any of the steps or the mayor made the choice public ... The e-mails, beginning in January 2013, highlight detailed conversations between Mayor Dave Bing's office, the Snyder administration, Kevyn Orr and Jones Day regarding bankruptcy." P. Jones, "Bankruptcy birthed in Snyder's office," *Michigan Citizen*, front page, July 25, 2013, "The city's bankruptcy affects all bond investments" and "Governor Snyder didn't explore . . . options. Instead he forced the city into bankruptcy . . . Snyder instead decided to play politics. His voting base are suburban wealthier citizens who don't have much at stake as far as Detroit is concerned—other than it being a place to go for entertainment or to commute to work."

Former Governor Snyder recently was forced to withdraw from an academic adjunct professorship by protest about his delays in addressing the water supply pollution of the Flint intake system from Lake Huron. Flint had chosen to break off from the Detroit-owned system and build its own facilities in hindsight to the detriment of the health of its residents. In trashing the revenue bond security of the Detroit Water System, neither Snyder, Orr, or Bing defended those bondholders who had provided the money to Detroit to maintain and upgrade that system to the highest code standards and even today think, without any market tested feasibility support, that regional control is the correct approach. The Flint disaster should have been the red light to stop undermining the credit of those bonds. David Eggbert, "Snyder withdraws from Harvard fellowship amid Flint backlash," *Washington Post*, July 3, 2019, *https://www.washingtonpost.com/national/higher-education/ ex-michigan-governor-turns-down-harvard-after-backlash/2019/07/03/ 0189eef2-9db5-11e9-83e3-45fded8e8d2e_story.html*.

[41] "The governor of debt-ridden Puerto Rico has hired the retired federal bankruptcy judge from Michigan who handled Detroit's historic bankruptcy for advice on shedding billions of dollars in debt . . . 'It's exactly like Detroit,' said Rhodes, who retired in February from the U.S. Bankruptcy Court in Detroit." Chad Livengood, "Rhodes on Puerto Rico: 'It's Exactly like Detroit,'" *The Detroit News*, June 29, 2015, *https://www.detroitnews.com/story/ news/local/detroit-city/2015/06/29/ex-bankruptcy-judge-rhodes-hired-advise- puerto-rico/29468203/*.

[42] Christine Ferretti, "Orr: Work still to be done in Detroit after the bankruptcy," *Detroit News*, January 27, 2015, *https://www.detroitnews.com/story/ news/local/wayne-county/2015/01/27/kevyn-orr-interview/22390837/*. See also previous endnote discussing the Flint water crisis.

[43] Rockefeller Philanthropy Advisors, "Detroit Grand Bargain." September 25, 2018.

[44] "Puerto Rico's governor, saying he needs to pull the island out of a 'death spiral,' has concluded that the Commonwealth cannot pay its roughly $72 billion in debts, an admission that will probably have wide-reaching financial repercussions." Michael Corkery and Mary Williams Walsh, "Puerto Rico's Governor Says Island's Debts Are 'Not Payable'" *N.Y. Times*, June 28, 2015, *https://www.nytimes.com/2015/06/29/business/dealbook/puerto-ricos-governor- says-islands-debts-are-not-payable.html*.

[45] "PROMESA," Wikipedia, *https://en.wikipedia.org/wiki/PROMESA*.

[46] "Senior bonds were only cut by 7%; that is, they will be able to recover 93% of the nominal value of the bonds, while the juniors were cut by 46.1%, enabling a recovery of only 53.9% of the bonds' nominal value. Ob-

viously, the weight of the cuts fell on the owners of junior bonds. It should be noted that Puerto Rican investors own a larger portion of these subordinated bonds." Abner Dennis, Kevin Connor, "The COFINA Agreement, Part 1: The First 40 Year Plan," Committee for Abolition of Illegitimate Debt, December 3, 2018, *http://www.cadtm.org/The-COFINA-Agreement-Part-1-The-First-40-Year-Plan.* For a discussion of who senior bondholders are, see Abner Dennis, Kevin Connor, "The COFINA Agreement, Part 2," Committee for Abolition of Illegitimate Debt, December 3, 2018, *http://www. cadtm.org/The-COFINA-Agreement-Part-2-Profits-for-the-Few.*

During the hearing, Judge Swain went as far as asking whether the island's Financial Oversight and Management Board intent, in seeking the confirmation of the COFINA debt deal, was to rewrite the Constitution. Plan proponents wanted the judge to agree that it was federal law and that its ancillary documents also had the force of law. "I don't think I am ready to do that," she said. Eva Llorens Velez, "Judge Swain Worries About Rewriting Puerto Rico's Constitution," *Caribbean Business,* January 17, 2019, *https:// caribbeanbusiness.com/judge-swain-worries-about-rewriting-puerto-ricos-constitution/.*

[48] That role was not necessary in New York and Connecticut. These states had political leaders willing to pay and not repudiate the debt, thereby protecting the basic asset of New York City, Yonkers, Buffalo, and Troy, the New York counties of Nassau and Erie, and the Connecticut cities of Bridgeport, Waterbury, East Haven, and, most recently, Hartford. In substance, those states chose not to allow repudiation of debt by a bankruptcy process; instead they chose to restructure the debt in a way that provided continued market acceptance for future capital infrastructure bonds. Similarly, Pennsylvania passed oversight statutes for Pittsburgh, Scranton, and Philadelphia and restructured debt rather than seek bankruptcy. Harrisburg did file because of a unique circumstance involving excess of debt in respect of a failed waste-to-energy plant.

[49] See e.g., *Politank Corp v. Aristela Capital LLC*, et al., U.S. Dist. Ct. P.R., Case 3:18-cv-01439-JAG, Complaint, filed 07/03/18 ¶11 (stating "COFINA Senior Bondholder Group were to pay . . . $55,000 a month") and ¶13 (stating "The agreement also provided for a success fee . . ." of $3,000,000 for a recovery of 95% or more), *https://media.noticel.com/o2com-noti-media-us-east-1/document_dev/2018/07/10/dem%20politank%20cabilderos_1531258631998_12345125_ver1.0.pdf*. See also Abner Dennis, Kevin Connor, "The COFINA Agreement, Part 2," Committee for Abolition of Illegitimate Debt, December 3, 2018, *http://www.cadtm.org/The-COFINA-Agreement-Part-2-Profits-for-the-Few*.

[50] "Critical Puerto Rico Infrastructure Left in Limbo," *Caribbean Business*, April 26, 2019, *https://caribbeanbusiness.com/critical-puerto-rico-infrastructure-projects-left-in-limbo/*.

[51] "The restructuring plan for what is known as COFINA debt carries grave consequences for the vast majority of Puerto Ricans: Money that could be funding health care, education, and a just recovery from 2017's hurricanes and a 13-year economic depression will instead pad the pockets of hedge-fund billionaires and their wealthy investors. Additionally, the deal is structured in a way that will deliver huge profits for vulture funds and significant losses for Puerto Rico–based investors, all the while being funded by one of the most regressive forms of tax there is—a sky-high sales tax, which at 11.5 percent is higher than in all 50 states." Abner Dennis and Kevin Conner, "Hedge Funds Win, Puerto Ricans Lose in First Debt Restructuring Deal," *The American Prospect*, February 5, 2018, *http://prospect.org/article/hedge-funds-win-puerto-ricans-lose-first-debt-restructuring-deal*. For the most critical and factually correct summary of Judge Swain's failure to appreciate the rights of the taxpayer to reemerge as "self-sufficient" from bankruptcy see Sergio Marxuach, "COFINA and the 'Good Enough' Restructuring Doctrine," Public Policy Director for the Center of a New Economy, February 12, 2019, *https://grupocne.org/2019/02/12/cofina-and-the-good-enough-restructuring-doctrine/*. Contrast this with the city of Yonkers, supra.

[52] "Sound the alarm bells! Puerto Rico is not just another one-off municipal finance catastrophe.

Without question, Puerto Rico's PROMESA-driven settlements, allegations of invalidity, and legal decisions weaken fundamental and long-standing protections of sources of payment and security of municipal debt." April 9, 2019 conference "Puerto Rico Bankruptcy Risk Summit, New York City" hosted by the Association of Financial Guaranty Insurers, and *Bond Buyer*.

[53] "The COFINA restructuring . . . saddles Puerto Rico with escalating debt payments for the next 20 years, even though the economy has been in a decade-long slump." Antonio Weiss, Brad W. Setser, and Desmond Lachman, "Puerto Rico Needs a Better Debt Deal," Bloomberg Opinion, October 8, 2018, *https://www.bloomberg.com/opinion/articles/2018-10-08/puerto-rico-needs-a-better-debt-deal.*

[54] "COFINA consisted of two distinct sets of bonds: the current interest bonds, and the capital appreciation bonds (the municipal bond market's version of zero coupon bonds). Before Maria, Puerto Rico was paying interest (at around 5.5 percent) on $12 billion or so of COFINA current interest bonds. But over time the COFINA capital appreciation bonds would mature, and thus total payments on the sales-tax backed COFINA bonds would rise from around $0.7 billion a year (1 pp of GNP) to $1.8 billion a year (around 2.5 pp of GNP, a sum that would essentially take up all of the 6 percentage points of Puerto Rico's sales tax pledged to back the bonds; in fact, it could have exceeded the pledge had Puerto Rico's economy continued to decline). Because of this structure, the burden created by the unrestructured COFINA structure was far larger than it seemed. And so too is the burden created by the agreed restructuring, as payments on the new COFINA bonds rise steadily over the next twenty plus years. Even after the restructuring, payments on the COFINA bonds would put Puerto Rico's debt burden (judged relative to its revenue) above that of an average state." Brad W. Setser, "Is There Still a Path that Returns Puerto Rico to Debt Sustainability?" Council on Foreign Relations, March 25, 2019, *https://www.cfr.org/blog/there-still-path-returns-puerto-rico-debt-sustainability.*

[55] Puerto Rico is currently running a cash surplus, thanks to the extra Medicaid funding Congress provided and the influx of tax revenues associated with federal disaster spending (contractors are reporting income in Puerto Rico, so corporate tax collections are up), so the real question is future not current payments capacity. Brad W. Setser, "Is There Still a Path that Returns Puerto Rico to Debt Sustainability?" Council on Foreign Relations, March 25, 2019, *https://www.cfr.org/blog/there-still-path-returns-puerto-rico-debt-sustainability.*

[56] Mary Williams Walsh, "Puerto Rico's Bankruptcy Plan Is Almost Done, and It Could Start a Fight," *N.Y. Times,* July 14, 2019, *https://www.nytimes.com/2019/07/14/business/puerto-rico-bankruptcy-promesa.html?smid=nyt-core-ios-share*

[57] "Public private partnerships (P3s) are contractual agreements between a public agency and a private entity that allow for greater private participation in the delivery of projects." U.S. Department of Transportation, "Public-Private Partnerships," *https://www.transportation.gov/buildamerica/programs-services/p3.*

[58] Later on, we learned a former attorney general of New Jersey was a partner at Skadden and was credited with bringing in the business.

[59] At a later time, the billings of the two firms became public. It was notable that the corporate firm had charged more than three times what the municipal firm charged.

[60] The growth of public authorities is documented in Robert Caro's book about Robert Moses. Mr. Delafield, of Hawkins, Delafield & Wood, was his lawyer and crafted the legislation and counseled the bonding for and by those authorities.

[61] "By 1970, the New Haven Water Company owned 25,000 acres of land in 17 south central Connecticut towns. Though primarily a supplier of water to the region, these vast real estate holdings had become invaluable resources as well. With the passage of the Safe Drinking Water Act in 1974, the company found itself subject to more stringent government regulations. To meet these costly requirements, it had to consider either selling off its real estate or raising water rates. The company opted to sell land. Because of objections from surrounding communities, a commission was formed to study the question. It was clear that the company could no longer remain in private hands. The commission recommended the formation of a publicly-owned regional water company. In 1977, the legislature created the South Central Connecticut Regional Water Authority to serve the area's recreational, environmental and water needs. The Regional Water Authority purchased the assets of the New Haven Water Company in 1980. The Authority's enabling legislation requires the Authority to provide an adequate supply of pure water at a reasonable cost while conserving land as open space and allowing compatible recreation use of land." Regional Water Authority, "Lifestream for a Region: History of the Regional Water Authority," *https://www.rwater.com/about-us/who-we-are/history-of-the-company.*

[62] Explaining all accounting differences between public authorities and the private corporations is beyond the scope of this book.

[63] Basically, this assumes that an entity will continue in business as a water-delivery entity charging fees based on water consumption for the foreseeable future.

[64] As underwriter's counsel, my tasks were to develop the offering document and do "due diligence" for that document.

[65] "To grasp the importance of this agreement it is necessary to understand some complicated history. New York City has long had the power to acquire property around the city's 19 reservoirs and to regulate development on adjacent lands. Because the city did not exercise that power for many years, local residents naturally got the idea that they could do whatever they liked. Development proceeded rapidly, first in Westchester County, later in Putnam County and now in the Catskills. Water quality declined, and in 1989 the Federal Government ordered the city to clean up the watershed or build a filtration plant it simply could not afford. The city then decided to enforce its powers, announcing that it would acquire thousands of acres of land to provide buffer zones around the reservoirs and writing new regulations governing sewage treatment plants and septic tanks. Upstaters bridled at these restrictions and filed one lawsuit after another. Not an acre of land was acquired, not a single sewage treatment plant upgraded. The watershed continued to deteriorate, and Washington renewed its threats." "At Last, a Watershed Agreement," *N.Y. Times* Op. Ed., November 3, 1995, *https:// www.nytimes.com/1995/11/03/opinion/at-last-a-watershed-agreement.html.*

[66] Details of the process are available in Michael C. Finnegan, "New York City's Watershed Agreement: A Lesson in Sharing Responsibility," *Pace Environmental Law Review* 14, no. 2 (June 1997), *https://digitalcommons.pace. edu/cgi/viewcontent.cgi?article=1486&context=pelr.* See also Jennifer Church, "Avoiding Further Conflict: A Case Study of the New York City Watershed Land Acquisition Program in Delaware County, NY," *Pace Environmental Law Review* 27, no. 1 (September 2009), *https://digitalcommons.pace.edu/cgi/ viewcontent.cgi?referer=https://www.google.com/&httpsredir=1&article=1012&- context=pelr.*

[67] On June 7, 1995, the General Assembly adopted Public Act 95-230, An Act to Enhance the Infrastructure of the University of Connecticut, now codified as Sections 10a-109a through 109y of the Connecticut General Statutes. When the final vote was cast for the act known as UConn2000, the renaissance of the University of Connecticut began.

On June 22, 1995, Governor John G. Rowland signed UConn 2000 into law at a ceremony in front on Babbidge Library, the symbol of the University's crumbling infrastructure. Through UConn2000, the executive and legislative branches addressed the university's need for a comprehensive infrastructure renewal program to attract Connecticut's high-achieving students, to educate a top-notch workforce, and to compete for job-creating research grants. The legislative program was designed to rebuild, restore, and enhance the university's physical infrastructure; it was also designed to enhance programmatic excellence by jumpstarting the University's private fundraising with an endowment matching grant program. The overwhelming bipartisan support for UConn 2000 reflected the depth of consensus regarding the goals as articulated in the law's statement of purpose. *UCONN 2000 Legislative Report No. 40;* UCONN 2000 Four Year Progress Report 1995–1999 Executive Summary.

[68] The statute pointed to the Connecticut Department of Public Works botching the Babbidge Library and that the department was already too busy on other state projects. "UConn's $1 billion responsibility," *Hartford Courant*, December 27, 1995.

[69] UCONN 2000 Legislative Report No. 40; UCONN 2000 Four-Year Progress Report 1995–1999 Executive Summary.

[70] "New York City produces more garbage than poetry. About 22,000 tons of it a day," *N.Y. Times* Op. Ed. "The Burning Garbage Issue," June 8, 1980.

[71] An overview and timeline can be found online. See Connecticut Resources Recovery Authority, "Timeline." *http://www.crra.org/pages/timeline.htm.*

[72] A history of Connecticut waste policy is available from Keila Torres Ocasio, "Twenty-Five Years of Trash to Energy," *CT Post*, June 17, 2013, *https:// www.ctpost.com/local/article/25-years-of-trash-to-energy-4604218.php.*

Recent decisions may put this practice in jeopardy. "Rising from the ashes are new plans developed by the Department of Energy & Environmental Protection to increase the recycling rate from 25 percent to 60 percent by 2024. How the rest of the trash is disposed still is a point of contention; the legislature is calling on DEEP to utilize some yet-to-be-determined technology with greater fiscal and environmental benefits. 'We don't want to set trash on fire anymore,' said Macky McCleary, DEEP deputy commissioner. 'Recycling has much more value to the system than incineration does.'" "CT Waste Future Leaves Trash-to-Energy In Dust," *Hartford Business*, June 2, 2014, *http://www.hartfordbusiness.com/article/20140602/PRINTEDITION/ 305309965/ct-waste-future-leaves-trash-to-energy-in-dust.*

[73] "In 1992, Kraft and Rand-Whitney announced plans to build a $125 million cardboard recycling plant on land purchased six years earlier in Montville. Kraft, who also bought two adjacent paper mills that employed about 300, said the new plant would create 80 additional jobs. The Krafts

found Connecticut, under the leadership of the business-friendly Weicker, receptive to their plans, something family members say they haven't always experienced in Massachusetts. The family applied for $30 million in tax-exempt industrial revenue bonds in June 1992, and the bonds were approved by the Connecticut Development Authority a month later." Greg Garber and Christopher Keating, "Kraft & Rowland: Maybe They Can Do Business," *Hartford Courant,* June 28, 1998, *http://articles.courant.com/1998-06-28/ sports/9806280155_1_robert-k-kraft-kraft-rowland-john-g-rowland.*

[74] "The author Tom Clancy is heading a major partnership interested in buying the New England Patriots and moving the team to Hartford, a Connecticut official said tonight." Associated Press, "Football; Clancy in Game for Patriots," *N.Y. Times,* January 13, 1994, *https://www.nytimes.com/ 1994/01/13/sports/football-clancy-in-game-for-patriots.html.*

[75] "Now the team will be on the move again, 85 miles away to Hartford. By 2001 at the earliest, the Patriots will move into a $375 million downtown stadium with 150 luxury suites and 5,000 club seats, thanks to a generous package approved Tuesday night by the Connecticut legislature. Some legislators complained about the generosity of the package." Richard Sandomir, "Early Football Patriots: Ragged, Proud, Broke," *N.Y. Times,* December 17, 1998, *https://www.nytimes.com/1998/12/17/nyregion/early-football-patriots-ragged-proud-broke.html.*

[76] "'Everybody thinks Robert Kraft came here to use us against Boston,' he said. But Ritter, then speaker of the House and key legislator in the renaissance of the University of Connecticut, spent a considerable amount of time with the Patriots owner—'he was extremely honorable,' Ritter said—adding that "Kraft was looking at houses in Connecticut as proof of his seriousness. Ritter says he believes the Connecticut deal fell apart because of factors outside of Kraft's control." John Altavilla and Daniela Altimari, "Hartford Patriots? It Seemed Too Good to be True," *Hartford Courant, February* 4, 2017, *http://www.courant.com/sports/football/hc-hartford-patriots-stadium-0205-20170204-story.html.*

[77] "Three major Hartford companies that have seen the value of their property plummet with the city's fortunes unveiled an ambitious $1 billion downtown development plan today that features a convention center and sports stadium. Still, no private money has been committed to the project, the largest proposed in Hartford in decades. The fact that it was conceived by the Phoenix Home Life Mutual Insurance Company, the Travelers Insurance Group and Connecticut Natural Gas, whose headquarters are all on or near

the site of the proposed project, has given the plan more credence than past proposals here." "A $1 Billion Development Is Proposed For Hartford," *N.Y. Times*, May 14, 1998, *https://www.nytimes.com/1998/05/14/nyregion/a-1-billion-development-is-proposed-for-hartford.html.*

[78] "Mr. Fiondella produced drawings that looked like a Tomorrowland vision of Hartford and began pointing to the features planned for Adriaen's Landing: a stadium for the Patriots and the University of Connecticut, a convention center, a hotel, a rooftop restaurant, a museum that looks like a solarium, an indoor mountain-climbing range, a jazz club, a 14-screen movie theater. Then they stepped to the window." Mike Allen, "Secret, Persistent Negotiations Lured the Patriots to Hartford," *N.Y. Times*, Nov. 22, 1998, *https://www.nytimes.com/1998/11/22/nyregion/secret-persistent-negotiations-lured-the-patriots-to-hartford.html.*

[79] "I want revenge—but can't figure out upon whom to direct it. Or how. How exactly do you vent on the gas people for having made such a mess of the deal? Possibly more than any other factor, the posturing and hardball negotiating of Arthur C. Marquardt from the gas company put the icepick into the spleen of this deal, which would have done so much for the city." Denis Horgan, "Robert Kraft Took Hartford On One Grand Ride," *Hartford Courant*, May 2, 1999, *http://articles.courant.com/1999-05-02/news/9905020111_1_gas-patriots-deal.*

[80] The 2015 movie *Spotlight* depicts some of this influence and power.

[81] "In 1994, Orthwein offered Kraft a $75 million buyout of his lease so he could move the team to St. Louis." Jackie MacMullan, "Robert Kraft Steady at the Helm," ABC News, January 15, 2014, *https://abcnews.go.com/Sports/robert-kraft-steady-helm/story?id=21542927.*

[82] The Constitution of the State of New York, Article X, Corporations, Section 5, "Public Corporations; restriction on creation and powers; accounts; obligations of" at *https://www.dos.ny.gov/info/constitution/article_10_corporations.html.*

[83] I knew Chester well from our work one long summer on the National Development Bank, an urban initiative, when he was an assistant secretary at the U.S. Department of the Treasury during the Carter administration.

[84] See previous endnote on support for UConn 2000.

[85] "[T]he State Constitution prohibits any public corporation from being given both the power to contract indebtedness and to collect fees for a

service formerly supplied by a City. These powers as they related to the New York City water and sewer system are, in fact, split between the Water Authority and the Water Board." Application of *Frederick Schmidt, et al v. Koch*, et al., Supreme Court (N.Y. 1989), at 13.

[86] "Where, as here, the statutory scheme stays within the letter of the Constitution (and carefully so, I believe) then we should heed Judge Desmond's statement in Comereski (308 NY 248, 254) that 'We should not strain ourselves to find illegality in such programs. The problems of a modern city can never be solved unless arrangements like these . . . are upheld, unless they are patently illegal. Surely such devices, no longer novel, are not more suspect now than they were twenty years ago when, in *Robertson v. Zimmerman* (268 NY 52, 62) we rejected a charge that this was a mere evasion of constitutional debt limitations, etc. Our answer was this (p. 65): "Since the city cannot itself meet the requirements of the situation, the only alternative is for the State, in the exercise of its police power, to provide a method of constructing the improvements and of financing their cost."'" *Wein v. City of New York*, 36 N.Y.2d 610, 620 (1975).

[87] "Lombard-Wall, collapsed in August 1982. Once again, Lombard-Wall had Repo transactions with the Street and with customers, but in this case, there was no large bank to cover the losses. Immediately following the bankruptcy, Lombard-Wall's Repo trades were tied up in bankruptcy court with no one allowed to liquidate them." Scott Skyrm (blog post), "Two Bankruptcies that Created the Modern Repo Market," *http://scottskyrm.com/ 2013/04/two-bankruptcies-that-created-the-modern-repo-market.*

[88] "Wall Street was shaken again yesterday by the failure of a little-known government securities firm, Lombard-Wall Inc., and its wholly owned subsidiary, Lombard-Wall Money Markets. In a bankruptcy petition, Lombard-Wall Inc. listed debts of $177.2 million to its 10 largest unsecured creditors. The two biggest were the Chase Manhattan Bank, which was owed $45 million, and the New York State Dormitory Authority, which was owed $55 million. The authority is a public agency that issues bonds to finance dormitory construction at state institutions." Robert J. Cole, "Wall St. Securities Firm Files For Bankruptcy," *N.Y. Times*, August 13, 1982, *https://www.nytimes. com/1982/08/13/business/wall-st-securities-firm-files-for-bankruptcy.html.*

[89] On August 12, 1982, the government securities trading firm of Lombard-Wall, Inc., filed for bankruptcy. The Corporation had invested approximately $130 million in "repurchase agreements" with Lombard-Wall at that time. Unlike other Lombard-Wall creditors, however, the Corporation had taken

a number of critical precautions to protect against just such an event including taking physical possession of the securities subject to repurchase, testing their market value on a daily basis, and insisting on the provision of letters of credit from a major commercial bank be available in any event of default. As a result of these precautions, the Corporation was able to secure full relief from the bankruptcy court by August 18. It had reinvested the proceeds (aided by the letters of credit) to assure the same future interest return as originally anticipated. On August 19, Moody's acted to suspend the ratings on every other revenue bond or note issue known to have had proceeds invested with Lombard-Wall (37 note and bond issues in all). HDC's notes alone were specifically reaffirmed at MIG-I. (*HDC Annual Report*, 1982).

[90] "The Chinese wall is a term describing an ethical barrier within an organization that prevents communication that creates conflicts of interest. For example, a Chinese wall could exist between departments where the exchange of information could unfairly influence trades. The 'wall' is figuratively erected to safeguard insider information and protect private data that could create negative implications and legal consequences if improperly shared." "What is a Chinese Wall?" Investopedia, *https://www.investopedia.com/terms/c/chinesewall.asp*.

[91] "Michele Sindona, the Italian financier who is serving a 25-year sentence in the United States for fraud, was extradited to Italy today to face new charges here." E. J. Dionne Jr., "Sindona is Extradited to Face Italian Charges," *N.Y. Times*, September 26, 1984, *http://www.nytimes.com/1984/09/26/business/sindona-is-extradited-to-face-italian-charges.html*.

[92] IRC Section 103 establishes state and local bond interest that is not included in gross income.

[93] "Bankruptcy Legend Harvey R. Miller Dies at 82", Weil.com, April 27, 2015, *https://www.weil.com/articles/bankruptcy-legend-harvey-r-miller-dies-at-82*.

[94] Washington Square Park, aside from the usual New York City distractions, has several granite chess tables in the park, offering those would-be lawyers who play chess "relief" from study.

[95] Holcomb Noble and Charles McGrath, "Louis Auchincloss, Chronicler of New York's Upper Crust, Dies at 92," *N.Y. Times*, Jan. 27, 2010, *http://www.nytimes.com/2010/01/28/nyregion/28auchincloss.html*.

[96] Photos of the devastation, particularly residential areas, are remarkable and are available online. The United States Geological Survey has some available at: *https://earthquake.usgs.gov/earthquakes/events/alaska1964/1964pics.php*.

[97] Wall Street is where George Washington took the oath of office as our first president and was home to the first Congress, Supreme Court, and Executive Branch offices.

[98] The majestic front door of the building still has preserved the bullet holes from the September 16, 1920, political terrorist bombing.

[99] Remember, this was before the 800-mile Alyeska pipeline was built to take advantage of the largest oil strike in the United States. It was discovered in 1968 underneath Prudhoe Bay and made Alaska a wealthy state.

[100] In these cases, "test" litigation challenging the validity of the statute (prepared by bond counsel and passed by the state) is filed by an actual taxpayer, who usually would be an employee of the law firm willing to prepare the complaint and brief challenging the statute.

[101] *Suber v. Alaska State Bond Committee,* 414 P.2d 546 (1966) is highly recommended reading for anyone wishing to understand public finance issues, including constitutional law related to statutes and regulations, liens and security interests, and legislative discretion, as well as state powers related to the police power, legislative enactment, executive power, limitations on funds or credit, and disbursements.

[102] For instance, during the 2016 period of fiscal chaos created by the governor of Puerto Rico, my 2006 financing structuring around a constitutional provision in Puerto Rico to securitize its new sales tax has been challenged. Hawkins issued a reasoned opinion that, in effect, stated that the substantial body of law on a comparable issue upheld in New York and other states would be treated as precedent by a federal or commonwealth court ruling on a complaint challenging the security structure of that bond. Since 2006, an additional fifteen billion bonds have been issued and supported by three successive Puerto Rico attorneys general and related subsequent bond and underwriter law firms using similar validating reasoned approving opinions based on prevailing precedents demonstrates favorable and reasonable legal analysis supportive of Hawkins original approving opinion. Yet the government of Puerto Rico, supported by the federally appointed oversight board, is now in court over the legality of those bonds.

[103] Bankruptcy courts don't usually review legality of issuance of bonds. The federal judges in Detroit made several rulings in that bankruptcy proceeding that have been well-criticized as simply wrong or not in the best interest of the Detroit taxpayers.

[104] "Whoops, or WPPSS, financed construction of five nuclear power plants by issuing billions of dollars in municipal bonds in the 1970s and 1980s. In 1983, because of extremely poor project management, construction on some plants was canceled, and completion of the remaining plants seemed unlikely. Consequently, the take-or-pay arrangements that had been backing the municipal bonds were ruled void by the Washington State Supreme Court. As a result, WPPSS had the largest municipal debt default in history." James Chen, reviewer, "Whoops," Investopedia, updated July 24, 2018, *https:// www.investopedia.com/terms/w/whoops.asp.*

[105] In the nineteenth century, issuers would bring the bonds to market and the banks would have their usual law firms review the documents prior to bidding. Almost always there would be a legal defect in the authorization process resulting in the issuer having to "do over" the process. So, the practice changed as issuers retained those bank firms to prepare the documents in the first place; hence, the dual role.

[106] "Historically, underwriters have required, as a condition to closing a registered offering of securities, that counsel provide them negative assurance regarding the disclosure in the registration statement and prospectus to help them establish due diligence under sections 11 and 12(a)(2) of the Securities Act of 1933 ('Securities Act'). Negative assurance is not a 'legal opinion.' Rather, it is a statement of belief, unique to securities offerings, based on participation in the intensive process of preparing, reviewing, and revising the registration statement and prospectus customarily conducted in connection with a registered offering." "Negative Assurance in Securities Offerings: Special Report of the Task Force on Securities Law Opinions, ABA Section of Business Law," *The Business Lawyer* 59 (August 2004) (internal references and citations omitted).

[107] "He also developed the concept of having municipalities issue tax-exempt bonds to finance the purchase of single-family homes and the use of floating rate tax-exempt financing." Alfonso A. Narvaez, "Walter J. Lopp 2d, 51, Banker and Corporate Finance Innovator" *N.Y. Times* obituary, August 15, 1990, *https://www.nytimes.com/1990/08/15/obituaries/walter-j-lopp-2d-51-banker-and-corporate-finance-innovator.html*

[108] Until Orange County, the only actual bond default that occurred during my practice happened in the Pacific Northwest under "whoops" or the Washington Public Power Supply System. The WPPSS was formed to ensure electrical power supply, but over the years WPPSS failed to successfully build and operate power generation plants, eventually defaulting on

$2.25 billion worth of bonds. Litigation followed. In *Chemical Bank (as trustee) v. Washington Public Power Supply System*, 102 Wa. 2d, 874, 691P. 2nd 329 (1984) the Washington Supreme Court held municipal "take or pay" energy purchase contacts invalid as creating unconstitutional debt, undermining the security for a material amount of bonds. Most commentaries believed the opinion upset the common practice of using "take or pay" contracts because WPPSS's (and the regions) economic circumstances had changed dramatically and the surrounding municipalities no longer needed the power generated by the plants built by from WPPSS issued bonds. See Andrew Beattie, "What Does 'WPPSS' Refer to in Muni Bond Defaults?" Investopedia, July 2, 2018, *https://www.investopedia.com/ask/answers/09/wpps-municipal-bond-default-whoops.asp.*

[109] In my view, nothing in the Dodd-Frank statute supports this requirement of a financial advisor and was simply a regulating insert by a creative lawyer from the staff of the S.E.C. imposing his own sense of safeguards. Such rule has seriously changed the ability of the issuers to receive confidential proposals from investment bankers. President Trump has vowed to pull back on many of the rules under that law.

[110] Many state laws and federal tax laws also allow tax deductions for donating and subjecting land to nondevelopment easements.

[111] "As outlined in the MSA, each of the Settling States gave up any future legal claims they might have based on the cigarette companies' actions at issue in the settled lawsuits . . . In exchange, the companies signing the MSA (the 'Participating Manufacturers') agreed to make annual payments in perpetuity to the Settling States to compensate them for taxpayer money spent for health-care costs connected to tobacco-related illness." Tobacco Control Legal Consortium, "The Master Settlement Agreement: An Overview." Pub. Health L. Center. *http://www.publichealthlawcenter.org/sites/default/files/resources/tclc-fs-msa-overview-2015.pdf.*

[112] "Fifteen years after tobacco companies agreed to pay billions of dollars in fines in what is still the largest civil litigation settlement in U.S. history, it's unclear how state governments are using much of that money. So far tobacco companies have paid more than $100 billion to state governments as part of the 25-year, $246 billion settlement." "15 Years Later, Where Did All The Cigarette Money Go?" NPR *All Things Considered*, October 13, 2013, *https://www.npr.org/2013/10/13/233449505/15-years-later-where-did-all-the-cigarette-money-go.*

Made in the USA
Monee, IL
31 October 2024

69064192R00115